CRE▲TIVE
HOMEOWNER®

Char-Broil®

grill yourself skinny

CREATIVE HOMEOWNER®, Mahwah, New Jersey

Char-Broil GRILL YOURSELF SKINNY

SUPERVISING EDITOR	Timothy O. Bakke
DESIGN AND LAYOUT	Scott Kraft
PRINCIPAL PHOTOGRAPHER	Glen E. Teitell, Freeze Frame Studio
FOOD STYLIST	Dyne Benner
DIGITAL IMAGING SPECIALISTS	Fred Becker, Segundo Gutierrez
INDEXER	Sandi Schroeder

Current Printing (last digit)
10 9 8 7 6 5 4

Manufactured in the United States of America

Grill Yourself Skinny
Library of Congress Control Number: 2011934457
ISBN-10: 1-58011-547-0
ISBN-13: 978-1-58011-547-6

CREATIVE HOMEOWNER®
A Division of Federal Marketing Corp.
One International Blvd., Suite 400
Mahwah, NJ 07495
www.creativehomeowner.com

Dedication: For Brad, whose taste buds will mature, I trust, as beautifully as the rest of him has.

And Jinny, who provides three of the most important ingredients when it comes to parenting: unwavering support, love, and encouragement.

Acknowledgments

First and foremost to Glen Teitell for recommending me for this project. To Brenda Beltram for introducing me to Glen. To Tim Bakke, who remains calm in the midst of (slight) chaos. To David, a dear friend who said, yes, of course you are doing this. To Daisy Pagani, who started out as an intern but is so stellar she moved to assistant rapidly. She was indispensible in helping get this book together. Watch out, Daisy is coming to prime time soon. To Todd Seyfarth, a talented teacher and chef, who is teaching a whole new generation the benefits of nutritional cuisine. To Nigel Morris, who is a true pleasure to do business with and who goes above and beyond to help. To Robert Schueller at Melissa's Produce, for answering questions and introducing me to the freshest fruit and vegetables, common and exotic, throughout the years.

To all of the Featured Chefs for their contributions. To Beth Schuben-Stein, who embraced the idea and contributed to it; Jen Burris, who helped with some research and compiling charts; Christopher Solga, who has also helped with research and compilations for this and other projects. Thank you to Karl Guggenmos, Lisa Young, Nancy Rodriguez, Chris Miller, and Steven Jenkins for their contributions.

To Michael, I would write something sentimental, but that is not my style. Jinny Skolnik, again, because she has been there again and again and again. Brad Skolnik, you rock! Neil Skolnik, because, after all, still.

— *Heidi*

All photography by
Freeze Frame Studio
except as noted.

Contents

4 Introduction

CHAPTER 1
18 BREAKFAST
Featured Chef: Jeff Mora

CHAPTER 2
34 APPETIZERS
Featured Chef: Peter Pahk

CHAPTER 3
52 SALADS
Featured Chef: Brad Farmerie

CHAPTER 4
68 SEAFOOD
Featured Chef: Dr. Christopher S. Ahmad

CHAPTER 5
88 POULTRY
Featured Chef: Angelo Basilone

CHAPTER 6
110 MEAT
Featured Chef: Graham Brown

CHAPTER 7
128 BURGERS & SLIDERS
Featured Chef: Todd Seyfarth

CHAPTER 8
142 VEGETABLES
Featured Chef: Todd C. Gray

CHAPTER 9
162 STARCHES
Featured Chef: Maxcel Hardy

CHAPTER 10
176 DESSERTS
Featured Chef: Elizabeth Karmel

188 Index

GRILL YOURSELF SKINNY?

OK, as a woman and a nutritionist, I actually dislike the word *skinny*. Maybe I should have used the word *trim* or *fit*? The real point here is that what you eat, when you eat, how much you eat, and the quality of those selections will determine, along with genetics and activity, your sustainable and realistic weight.

Grilling is a healthy, lean way to prepare food and is actually the perfect medium to use when trying to lose or maintain a healthy weight. Grilled fare is typically whole, unprocessed, unadulterated food that sustains, satisfies, and fulfills us.

When you grill, all you have to do is follow some simple guidelines, and you will have complete meals that will keep you on track to meeting your weight and health goals:

- Select lean versus higher-fat cuts of meat.
- Throw in some wonderful marinades, rubs, and spices.
- Use a range of vegetables.
- Choose healthy fats, such as olive oil.
- Experiment with some fruits.
- Add grilled ingredients to healthy grains.

Contemporary Grilling

A typical old-fashioned barbecue meal can easily add up to over 2,200 calories, more than a day's worth of calories for most people in one meal. (See "This Ain't Your Daddy's BBQ," page 5.)

Welcome to now: the contemporary world of grilling, where lean, healthy ingredients and an array of flavors combine. The new and improved—leaner—grill cuisine allows you to use this simple method of preparation year-round.

The menu used to illustrate the better BBQ in "This Ain't Your Daddy's BBQ" is still too much food for anyone trying to lose or manage his or her weight. A more-realistic menu would include an appetizer or salad, a protein entrée, a vegeta-

ble, and a small starch portion. (See "Skinny Menu and Calorie Count," page 5.) If you are drinking or having dessert, you may want to keep the carbohydrates (starchy selections) to a minimum. What you choose as an appetizer—protein-based or starchy—will have an impact on what you choose as your entrée and side. Going with a carb-heavy appetizer? Choose more protein and vegetables for your main meal. Choosing protein for your appetizer? Then go for a main meal that has some carbohydrates/starch. There is no way around portions. (See "Portion Distortion," page 17.)

Lean Ground Pork with Asian Slaw , page 135

Recipes

Each recipe includes ingredients, preparation, and grilling directions, as well as a breakdown on calories and grams of protein, carbohydrate, fat, and fiber, plus important nutrients. Of course, how much you eat and how you put together a meal will ultimately influence the bottom line. I share some tips on how you can use the recipes to put together a complete, satisfying, and calorie-sensible meal. You will also find out the "Nutrition 4-1-1" on some of the ingredients used in the recipes.

Each section of recipes begins with a **Featured Chef** who has provided, along with a great-tasting recipe, an insider's look at one wellness behavior they use to keep balanced and healthy in their own lives. All of the recipes are chef-developed, some more traditional with a healthier and lighter twist, others a bit more contemporary, which may stretch your palate. There are so many wonderful, healthy foods out there: find the ones that make your toes curl, and enjoy every (portion-managed) bite!

This Ain't Your Daddy's BBQ

When I was growing up—and even now, depending on who is hosting—a barbecue meant ribs, hot dogs, buttered corn, and accoutrements like potato salad swimming in mayonnaise and dessert: pie with ice cream.

I loved those barbecues because they usually meant summer mixed with family or friends. Well, welcome to the 21st century. Saving the grill for summer or parties is a thing of the past. My childhood view of good food has also been redefined.

Check out the comparison (above and at right) to see how delicious and slimming a *Grill Yourself Skinny* barbecue can be.

By grilling up some of the delicious and healthier recipes in this book, almost 1,500 calories were saved versus a typical old-fashioned BBQ. But really, no one is getting skinny by either menu: over 1,000 calories are still too many calories for one meal, and what is illustrated above is still too much food. Keep reading to find out better ideas on how to select and balance the right amount of food to keep your grilled meals satisfying to both your appetite and your waistline.

Old-Fashioned BBQ	Calories	*Grill Yourself Skinny* BBQ	Calories
Iceberg lettuce, 2 tablespoons ranch dressing	180	3 grilled mushroom lettuce wraps	80
3 ribs	435	2 grilled Cervena venison chops	280
1 hot dog	381	Sea bass with tropical salsa	130
1 cheeseburger	550	1 turkey-cranberry slider with green bean pesto	140
Macaroni salad (½ cup)	135	Quinoa and grilled vegetables (½ cup)	140
Buttered corn on the cob, 3 pats of butter	170	Sweet corn with red pepper, cilantro, and lime (½ cup)	105
Baked beans (½ cup)	140	Caraway-flavored baby bok choy	20
Apple pie à la mode	550	Grilled-peach melba	170
TOTAL CALORIES	**2541**		**1065**

Does not include sweet tea, lemonade, beer, or mixed drinks

SKINNY MENU AND CALORIE COUNT

Grill Yourself Skinny BBQ	Calories
3 grilled mushroom lettuce wraps	80
Sea bass with tropical salsa	130
Sweet corn with red pepper, cilantro and lime (½ cup)	105
Caraway-flavored baby bok choy	20
TOTAL CALORIES	**335**

Weight Loss Is (Not) Easy

Do not let anyone fool you: weight loss isn't easy. It takes thought, planning, and often relearning how to approach eating and food selection. It may require modifying when you eat and when you stop eating; it may entail looking at a food-abundant gathering a bit differently than you have in the past — more like skills that need to be mastered before they seem effortless. In the pages that follow, you will find insights to help you develop skills so that you can reach and maintain a weight that is right for your body.

— *Heidi*

Sea Bass with Tropical Salsa, page 78

Getting Started

Housework is not my thing, but I would be remiss if I did not share—before we really get going here—some tips on how to clean and maintain your grill, as well as a few food-safety thoughts. You'll also find in this section

- Tips for marinades and rubs
- A guide to knives
- Tips on beverages and weight loss
- A look at protein
- A discussion about portions

Grill Basics

We've all heard the saying "An ounce of prevention is worth a pound of cure." This is great advice when it comes to maintaining your grill.

Traditional Gas Grills. Periodic cleaning is necessary, as grill fires can occur when grease and food debris collect in the bottom of the grill. After each use, remove any remaining food particles from the cooking grate and inside the grill using a grill brush. Do this after the grill has cooled down yet is still warm. Traditional gas grills are not designed to be "burned off" by closing the lid and turning the burners on high for an extended time. The excessive heat generated can cause leftover grease to catch fire and can cause permanent damage to your grill.

Infrared Grills. The more you use most Infrared grills the better they will cook. The darker, or "more seasoned," the cooking grates become, the hotter and more evenly the unit will cook. It does require some maintenance to keep the grill performing at its peak.

- After each use, burn off any excess grease and food debris that has accumulated. Turn grill to high, and close the lid. Leave it on for around 15 minutes, and this should turn the debris to ash.
- After the grill has cooled down but is still warm, clean the cooking grates with a heavy-duty grill brush.
- Lastly, apply (brush or spray) a light coat of high-heat cooking oil to the grates to keep the surface seasoned.

General Grill Cleaning

- Plastic parts: wash with warm soapy water, and wipe dry. Do not use abrasive cleaners, degreasers, or a concentrated grill cleaner on plastic parts.
- Porcelain surfaces: because of porcelain's glass-like composition, you can wipe away most residues using a baking soda/water solution or glass cleaner. Use non-abrasive scouring powder for stubborn stains.
- Painted surfaces: wash with mild detergent or non-abrasive cleaner and warm water. Wipe dry with a soft non-abrasive cloth.
- Stainless-steel surfaces: stainless steel can rust under certain conditions. This can be caused by environmental conditions, such as chlorine or salt water, or using improper cleaning tools, such as wire or steel wool. It can also discolor due to heat, chemicals, or grease buildup. To maintain your grill's appearance, wash it with mild detergent and warm water, or use a stainless-steel grill cleaner. Baked-on grease deposits may require the use of an abrasive plastic cleaning pad. Use it only in the direction of the brushed finish to avoid damage. Do not use abrasive pads on areas with graphics.

Quinoa and grilled vegetables, page 169

- Cooking surfaces: if you use a bristle brush to clean cooking surfaces, ensure that no loose bristles remain on the surfaces prior to grilling. Do not clean cooking surfaces while the grill is hot.

Storing Your Grill
- Clean the cooking grates.
- Store the grill in a dry location.
- When the liquid propane (LP) cylinder is connected to the grill, store it outdoors in a well ventilated space and out of reach of children.
- Cover the grill if you store it outdoors. Choose from a variety of weather-resistant grill covers offered by the manufacturer.
- Store the grill indoors only if you have turned off, disconnected, and removed the LP cylinder from grill. Never store an LP cylinder indoors.

Critters/Insects
Spiders like to make their homes in the venturi tubes of grills. Inspect and clean them regularly to ensure that there are no blockages.

Food Safety

I think we can all agree, getting family and guests sick is never a good recipe for a fun night! Below are some basic and easy reminders about grilling and food safety as recommended by the United States Department of Agriculture.

- **Clean** hands and food surfaces before and after handling food.

- **Cross-contamination:** avoid it! Once a utensil or surface (plate, counter, and the like) comes in contact with raw meat, poultry, or seafood, you must clean it. If you slice meat with a knife and use that same knife to slice through a head of lettuce without cleaning it, the lettuce could then carry bacteria that could, because the lettuce will not be cooked and the bacteria killed, cause food-borne illness. That goes for marinades, too. Save some fresh marinade if you want to use it after the food is cooked. Throw out any marinade in which

WHAT TO LOOK FOR WHEN BUYING A GRILL

According to a national survey, Americans grill twice a week or more. With all of that use, it's no wonder that the average grill is replaced about every five years. If the last time you updated your grill was before beer-can chicken became popular, then prepare to be pleasantly surprised. Grills today come with accessories and innovations that help you make the most of your multi-year investment. Whether you're shopping based on budget, brand, or the goal of simply cooking better food, here are some tips straight from industry experts.

A new set of standards
Charcoal grills still have a big following, but the convenience of gas grills has made them the most popular choice in America. And be aware, small electric grills are on the horizon for high-rises and other restricted spaces. The first thing you'll find as you shop is that the traditional gas grill, which heats the air and tends to dry out food, is becoming obsolete.

Today, new infrared grills are the latest innovation in the market because they

- Prevent flare-ups.
- Deliver even heat across the grill grates, with no hot or cold spots.
- Promise much juicier foods.
- Deliver greater fuel efficiency.
- Provide the widest infrared temperature range.

No matter what type of grill you choose, features like the following can make your grilling experience easy and more enjoyable:
- Electronic ignition system, for easy starting
- Porcelain-coated cast-iron cooking grates, for easy cleanup and great results
- The option to cook with propane or natural gas
- Warming racks

And don't forget the huge array of accessories available today. Griddles, baskets, steamers, or skewer sets can help you prepare a greater variety of foods, even eggs and bacon for breakfast.

As you shop all the options, one thing is for sure, there's a whole lot to love about grilling today – most importantly the good times together with family and friends.

you soaked raw meat, fish, or poultry. Never mix cooked and raw foods.

• **Cook through:** Outside grill marks do not ensure that a food is cooked through and has reached a safe minimum internal temperature to kill harmful bacteria. Steaks, roasts, and chops should be cooked to at least 145°F. Hamburgers should reach 160°F. All poultry should reach a minimum of 165°F. Fish should be cooked to 145°F. Fully cooked meats like hot dogs should be grilled to 165°F or until steaming hot.

• **Chill:** Now when I say chill, I am not referring to kicking back and enjoying the food. That comes later. The chill I am referring to is the old adage, "keep cold foods cold and hot foods hot." Leaving foods out for long periods of time either before you are ready to grill or after you have cooked but are not ready to clean up can be a concern from a food-safety perspective. Use ice packs to keep cold food cold, or take it out just before you need it. Put food away as soon as you are finished eating, or throw it out after it has been prepared if it has been sitting out for more than two hours. It may still seem "fresh" to you, but the bacteria that causes illness has been growing while you have been chillin'. (A great resource is http://www.fsis.usda.gov/pdf/barbecue_food_safety.pdf.)

Marinades, Rubs—Rules of Thumb

By Karl Guggenmos WACS Global Master Chef
University Dean of Culinary Education for Johnson & Wales University

For centuries, cooks have used a variety of techniques to enhance the flavor and texture of foods that they prepare. Marinades and early forms of rubs, primarily salt, were originally used for preservation. Fish and meat were air-dried and then heavily salted, and thereby preserved. Marinades, especially pickling techniques, were used to preserve vegetables and fruits. Over the years, cooks discovered that applying acidic marinades to

Skirt Steak with Pepper Chimichurri Sauce, page 120

MARINADE & RUB DOS AND DON'TS

Do blanch vegetables before rubbing or marinating.
Do choose mild herbs and spices.
Do spread rubs evenly over the whole product.
Do taste your rub or marinade before applying it. If it's too strong or weak, you can correct it before finishing the process.
Do use the right temperature: high for meats; medium to low for seafood and vegetables

Don't overpower your food: cooks often add too much or too strong a flavor to the food they are cooking, especially seafood.

Don't marinate or rub too early before cooking, especially when cooking seafood and vegetables. Prolonged marinating or resting food after applying a rub results in loss of moisture and a dried texture after cooking. For best results, marinate single portions of seafood and vegetables no more than 30 minutes before grilling; marinate single portions of steaks no more than 1 hour beforehand. The exceptions to this are large cuts of meats, whole poultry, and whole fish. The best time for large meat cuts and whole poultry, for example, is 24–36 hours.

certain tough cuts of meat had a tenderizing effect. In recent times, the application of rubs and marinades has become very popular, primarily because it adds exciting flavors.

During my career I have used—and still use—dry rubs, wet rubs, marinades, and brines to add great flavors—and in some cases to reduce undesirable ones. Red-wine-based marinades, for example, reduce the "gamey flavor" of game meat. Another good reason for rubs is the health benefit derived from the various herbs and spices used in them. (See "Health Benefits of Spices," on page 10)

• **Dry rubs** can contain a variety of seasoning herbs and spices, applied (rubbed) onto meats and seafood prior to grilling. They enhance or bring out the flavor of the item to be cooked.

• **Wet rubs** are created by adding oil or another wet substance (paste) to a dry rub.

• **Marinades** consist of spices, herbs, and flavor-enhancing liquids such as fruit juices, sauces, oils, wines, vinegars, and even dairy. I also use marinating liquid to make sauce when roasting or grilling. Adding sweet ingredients to a marinade will help caramelize and crisp grilled meats.

• **Brines** are salt-based solutions that help meats keep their moisture so that they stay juicy during grilling. They are popular for poultry and lean meats. Herbs, spices, and sweets like honey can be added for additional flavor. When using brines, make sure the food is completely immersed. (Some prefer to inject brines into whole poultry.) Make sure that you rinse the food before grilling.

Ostrich Open-Faced Sandwich with Sundried Tomatoes and Chimichurri Sauce, page 108

Roasted-Garlic-and-Balsamic-Marinated Vegetable Kebabs, page 152

HEALTH BENEFITS OF SPICES — ENHANCE YOUR FLAVOR!

In addition to using herbs and spices as parts of rubs and marinades, check out their benefits and some other ways that you can use them.

Spice	Serving size	ORAC*	Proposed Health Benefits	Try it out!
Cinnamon	1 tsp	3417	May lower blood sugar, triglycerides, and LDL-cholesterol in people with type 2 diabetes	Sprinkle cinnamon in your oatmeal, or dip berries into yogurt sweetened with cinnamon.
Turmeric	½ tsp	1398	Turmeric contains curcumin, which is a member of the ginger family. May inhibit the growth of cancer cells, help manage IBS symptoms, and promote brain health.	Add turmeric to water when cooking brown rice, or add to egg or tuna salad.
Cayenne	1 tsp	638	Cayenne is sometimes referred to as "crushed red pepper" and is the main ingredient in chili powder. May help increase metabolism and aid mild indigestion.	Try adding cayenne to spice up your tomato sauces, soups, hummus, fish, or marinades.
Oregano	½ tsp	1598	Oregano is among the highest antioxidants of all herbs; however, no clinical studies have proven specific health benefits.	Add oregano to pasta sauce or sprinkle onto a grilled cheese sandwich.
Ginger	1 tsp	703	Ginger may help decrease motion sickness, nausea, morning sickness during pregnancy, and pain from arthritis. Be sure to talk to your doctor before surgery or if you are taking blood thinners or aspirin.	Try adding ground ginger to vegetables or using fresh ginger root in tea.
Paprika	1 tsp	504	Paprika contains an antioxidant and anti-inflammatory agent called capsaicin, which may help decrease risk of cancer.	Try adding paprika with thyme and red pepper to spice up your popcorn or adding paprika to lean meat.
Rosemary	1 tsp	1983	Rosemary has antimicrobial properties and has shown potential to decrease inflammation and aid in dyspepsia. There is weak evidence that it may have anticancer properties. **WARNING!** Pregnant women should not take large doses.	Add rosemary to whole-grain rolls and bread, tomato sauces, and grilled potatoes.
Saffron			May lift your mood and treat depression.	Try seeping saffron into tea or in water to prepare brown rice.
Garlic	1 tsp (powder)	207	May help decrease cholesterol and triglycerides. There is some evidence garlic may help decrease blood pressure in hypertensive individuals as well as repel insects. **WARNING!** Use caution if you are taking insulin or if you are on a anticoagulant	Add to sauces or marinades.

*Oxygen radical absorbance capacity (ORAC) is a method developed by the National Institute on Aging in the National Institutes of Health (NIH) of measuring *antioxidant* capabilities in a food. A high ORAC value indicates a high amount of antioxidants in the food. Antioxidants are the helpful vitamins, minerals, and enzymes in your body that minimize damage caused by free radicals, which are created during oxidation, when molecules in your body become damaged and lose an electron. Antioxidants help heal that damage.

A WORD ABOUT KNIVES

By Karl Guggenmos WACS Global Master Chef
University Dean of Culinary Education for Johnson & Wales University

The knife is one tool that gets chefs and home cooks equally excited and divided. You can spend a fortune on knives of all sorts, but really there are only a few that we use all of the time. Here are my recommendations of knives that you must have; all others are just nice to own (and show off):

• *French,* or *chef's, knife* comes in lengths of anywhere from 8–14 inches. I recommend 10 inches. Use it for major cutting, chopping, and dicing.

• *Utility knife* is smaller and lighter, 5–7 inches at the blade. It is ideal for smaller hands and versatile enough for a majority of cutting techniques.

• *Santoku knife* is a very popular knife. Japanese by origin, it is use just for chopping, dicing, and mincing. Some chefs use a Santoku knife exclusively. It typically has a 5–7-inch blade and is known for its sharpness; beveled, or hollow, ground; and scalloped edge, which helps release sticky food and slices after cutting.

• *Slicer* is a serrated long, narrow knife, with its blade 12 inches or longer. Use it for slicing crusty foods, breads, and roast.

• *Paring knife* is a short, pointed knife, about 2–4 inches in length. Use it for peeling, trimming, and paring vegetables and fruits.
(Note: For the grill cook, a braising fork, tongs, and spatula will also be helpful.)

Using knives the right way
• Hold the knife firmly by the handle only.
• Use the right knife for the right task.
• Always hold the blade down while walking with a knife.
• Always use a cutting board.
• Always use a sharp knife.
• Never try to catch a falling knife.
• Always wash and sanitize the knife after each use.
• Sharpen the blade with appropriate tools. (Note: using a steel does not sharpen a blade, it just keeps the edge straight, allowing it to cut better. You need a rotating stone sharpener to actually keep the blade sharp.)
• Do not leave knives in standing water.
• Do not clean knives in the dishwasher. The chemicals are just too strong.

Beverages and Weight Loss

Alcoholic Drinks. Thinking party? What is the harm of two cool, refreshing piña coladas to go with the fun, friends, and food at your backyard bash? Let's say you need 1,800 calories to maintain your weight and 1,500 calories to lose weight. Before you even begin eating, your alcoholic beverage of choice rakes up 874 calories, or 58% of your total caloric needs for the day!

If weight loss is your aim, skip the frozen umbrella drink and go with a simple red or white wine, sipped leisurely with your *Grill Yourself Skinny* meal.

Here are some other ways consuming too many alcoholic drinks can sabotage weight loss efforts:
• Less inhibited about what and how much you eat
• Interferes with sleep—and being tired can interfere with appetite-regulating hormones, increasing the risk of confusing tired with being hungry and increasing the risk of overeating the next day
• Interferes with sleep and, therefore, recovery (and muscle building) from exercise
• Can throw off your blood sugar the following day, thereby increasing cravings

Sip away if you'd like, enjoying the food and conversation. Just remember that if you drink, do so mindfully and within the parameters that match your goals.

Merlot
5 oz., 119 Cal.

Chardonnay
5 oz., 120 Cal.

Champagne
4 oz., 105 Cal.

Port
3.5 oz., 165 Cal.

Miller Light
12 oz., 96 Cal.

Guinness
12 oz., 125 Cal.

Blue Moon
12 oz., 164 Cal.

Sierra Pale Ale
12 oz., 175 Cal.

Margarita
8 oz., 371 Cal.

Piña Colada
8 oz., 437 Cal.

	Serving (oz.)	Calories
Merlot	5	119
Chardonnay	5	120
Champagne	4	105
Port	3.5	165
Miller Light	12	96
Guinness Draught	12	125
Blue Moon	12	164
Sierra Nevada Pale Ale	12	175
Margarita	8	371
Piña Colada	8	437
Daiquiri	8	229
Cosmopolitan	5	150
Long Island Iced Tea	8.3	276
Gin & Tonic	12	230
Vodka & Club Soda	12	97

Non-Alcoholic Drinks. When trying to lose weight, *do not drink your calories in the form of sugar-laden, nutrient-empty drinks.*
• They may keep your sweet cravings going.
• They will not fill you up as food does because beverages do not register the same as solid foods or even soup.

It is not just the colas; sweetened iced teas, lemonades, and vitamin-infused waters can all add up. Check the ingredients on the label (and the table at right).

The first two ingredients in all of the above mentioned:
   Cola: water, cane sugar (or corn syrup)
   Iced tea: tea, cane sugar (or corn syrup)
   Lemonade: water, sugar
   Vitamin water: crystalline fructose, cane sugar

For the same or fewer calories than 20 ounces of sweet tea, you could have any one of the *Grill Yourself Skinny* desserts (pages 176–187) or full entrees like Artic Char with Pepper Guacamole (p. 72), Tandoori Spice-Rubbed Chicken (p. 96), Filet Mignon with Red-Grape Sauce (p. 118)

Healthy Alternatives. So what can you drink when water seems boring?
• Fresh mint leaf and lemon added to a pitcher of water
• Herbal teas—hot or cold
• Unsweetened teas with fresh lemon
• Flavored seltzers
• 1 part real fruit juice mixed with 3 parts seltzer for a carbonated delight

And if you really want to add sugar, go ahead, but taste along the way. You may be surprised that you can add much LESS than that which is in the presweetened beverages that you buy.

	Arizona Lemon Iced Tea	Snapple Lemonade	Cola	Vitamin Water
Serving size (oz.)	20	16	20	20
Calories	255	190	240	125
Fat (g)	0	0	0	0
Cholesterol (mg	0	0	0	0
Carbohydrates (g)	62.5*	47*	66*	32.5*
Sugars (g)	60	46	66	32.5
Fiber (g)	0	0	0	0
Protein (g)	0	0	0	0

*4.4 grams = 1 teaspoon of sugar.

Daiquiri
8 oz., 229 Cal.

Cosmopoltian
5 oz., 150 Cal.

Long Island Iced Tea
8.3 oz., 276 Cal.

Gin & Tonic
12 oz., 230 Cal.

Vodka & Club
12 oz., 97 Cal.

Snapple Lemonade
16 oz., 190 Cal.

Cola
20 oz., 240 Cal.

Vitamin Water
20 oz., 125 Cal.

Arizona Lemon Iced Tea
20 oz., 225 Cal.

PROTEIN AND WEIGHT LOSS

By Nancy R. Rodriguez, PhD, RD, CSSD, FACSM

Professor, Nutritional Sciences, University Teaching Fellow

Director, Sports Nutrition Programs, University of Connecticut

Adding dietary protein to meals can enhance weight-management and health outcomes. Benefits attributed to increasing good-quality protein intake in each meal include satiety, weight loss, less fatigue, and improved metabolic profiles, suggesting less risk for cardiovascular disease and diabetes. Good-quality proteins include dairy products, meat, poultry, seafood, and for non-meat eaters, soy products like tofu. The beauty of these protein sources is their nutrient density. For reasonably few calories, you get lots of essential nutrients, vitamins, and minerals, so by incorporating protein into every meal, you eat healthfully. The simple addition of protein (like eggs) to breakfast increases satiety, so you're likely to consume fewer calories at lunch. Similarly, routine consumption of protein throughout the day has been shown to decrease calorie intake and lead to weight loss. Other benefits: improved cognition and less perceived fatigue. The extra protein optimizes weight loss by promoting the loss of fat while maintaining muscle. For individuals with high blood pressure, elevated cholesterol, or poor glucose control, habitually eating protein at meals and for snacks throughout the day may assist with reductions in blood pressure and cholesterol, as well as improve blood glucose control.

AAS Guide to Macronutrient Intake

Total Calories in Diet	Percent Total Calories		
	45%–65% CARB (g)	10%–35% PROTEIN (g)	20%–35% FAT(g)
1,200	135–195	30–105	27–47
1,400	158–228	35–123	31–54
1,500	169–244	38–131	33–58
1,800	203–293	45–158	40–70
2,000	225–325	50–175	44–78
2,200	248–358	55–193	49–86
2,500	281–406	63–219	56–97

Serving Sizes

Food	Visual Cue
1 cup broccoli	1 baseball
½ cup sliced fruit; 1 small apple or orange	1 tennis ball
½ cup pasta, rice, or cereal; ½ bagel	1 hockey puck
1 slice whole grain bread; 1 pancake	1 CD case
3 oz. meat	1 deck of cards
4 oz. fish	1 checkbook
1 tsp. butter or margarine	1 postage stamp
1 oz. cheese	2–4 dice
2 tbs. peanut butter	1 golf ball

**Portion Control—Plate Method
(Use 8–9-in. plate as main plate.)**

4-8 oz. low fat dairy

4 oz. fruit (1 medium fruit)

¼ plate starches = ½ cup

½ plate vegetables = 1–2 cups

¼ plate protein = 4 oz.

What's in a Portion?

You don't need to eat out to engage in portion distortion. Learn healthier portion sizes to help you serve up the right amount for you and your family at home. It seems a bit much to weigh and measure everything we eat; however, it can be a great exercise to try at least once to see whether, when you are "eyeballing" ½ cup of rice, for example, you are even close or not. One research study asked trained nutrition professionals (dietitians) to guess at the calories and fat in a number of meals, and even they underestimated the number of calories by 37 percent and amount of fat by 49 percent. Look at the table opposite ("Serving Sizes") for a handy reference of portion sizes.

However, we also know that not everyone has the same food preferences or style of eating. The American Academy of Sciences (AAS) recognizes that there is a range of values for macronutrients that you can consume as part of a healthy diet. (See the table opposite.) For weight loss, for example, you may do better with a slightly higher protein intake and a slightly smaller starch intake. Or

if a Mediterranean style of eating suits you and your health goals, your fat intake may be as high as 40 percent (but from healthy fats like olive oil, avocado, nuts, and fatty fish). Mediterranean-style eating is extremely healthy for everything from maintaining healthy blood pressure to a reduced risk of heart disease and diabetes.

You will see nutritional analyses in each recipe that follows in this book. The idea is not necessarily to eat the fewest calories or fat or protein or carbohydrate, per se, but to put together balanced, satisfying meals. Balance appetizers with entrées and sides. Perhaps leave off a side starch if you choose an appetizer that is higher in carbohydrate or choose a higher protein appetizer if your entrée is higher in carbohydrate or low in protein. Skip the appetizer if you are going to have a drink, or skip the drink if you are going to have dessert. In the end, it will come down to selecting the overall appropriate portion size for your weight goal, taking into account how much activity you do, your weight and appetite histories, genetics, and all the factors that drive us to eat.

Overcoming Portion Distortion: Learn to SMARTSIZE!

By Lisa R. Young, PhD, RD

Many restaurant food portions are now two to five times larger than they were in the past. *Mega size, king size, double gulp, triple burgers . . .* these are just a few descriptors you will see on a menu (usually fast-food).

- Typical bagels have doubled in size and are now equivalent to eating five slices of bread.
- A steak in a steakhouse may be so big that it is the equivalent in protein to eating 18 eggs.
- A bag of popcorn at the movies was once 5 cups; now a "bucket" can contain 20 cups.

With the focus on putting a stop to increasing obesity rates in both adults and children, one would hope that food companies had begun to scale back on portions; however, just the opposite appears to be happening.

Why should we care about large portions? Because without even realizing it, we tend to eat more—and therefore more calories—when served large portions. While an 8-ounce soda contains 100 calories, a 20-ounce bottle that you commonly get from a vending machine contains 250 calories. A small order of French fries at McDonald's contains 210 calories, while a large order packs in over 500 calories. The original Whopper, Burger King's signature hamburger sandwich, was introduced with a single ¼-pound beef patty at 670 calories; today's Triple Whopper with cheese packs in 1,250 calories.

What can we do about large portions? Learn to *smartsize!* One of my favorite food facts is that

you can lose 10 pounds a year by cutting back 100 calories a day. That's a few fewer bites of a dessert, a handful less of potato chips, or a couple of fork-twirls less of pasta. To trim calories, just trim your portions.

Here are some examples of small lifestyle changes that you can live with:

- Split a small order of French fries with a friend.
- Switch from a 20-ounce bottle of soda to a 12-ounce can. Better yet, switch to water or unsweetened flavored seltzer.
- Eat only one-half of a candy bar or one-half of an energy bar.
- Use a single tablespoon of salad dressing instead of two.
- Split your favorite dessert three ways.

These tips can help you smartsize your portions when dining out, supermarket shopping, or eating at home:

- Order "appetizer" portions or "half-size" portions.
- Share an entrée.
- Order salad dressings and sauces on the side.
- Buy single-serving portions whenever possible.
- Read food labels. Check for the number of servings per container.
- At home, don't eat directly from the refrigerator or while preparing food.
- At the end of your family meal, wrap up leftovers immediately.
- Learn to cook. Measuring out ingredients gives you a feel for food size.

Lisa R. Young, PhD, RD is the author of The *Portion Teller Plan: The No-Diet Reality Guide to Eating, Cheating, and Losing Weight Permanently*. A nationally recognized nutritionist, Dr. Young maintains a private practice in New York, NY. She is also an adjunct professor of nutrition at New York University. For more information, visit www.portionteller.com.

PORTION DISTORTION – HOW HUNGRY ARE YOU?

When you choose the larger portion when a smaller one will do, do you realize how much more work you are creating for yourself— your body— to maintain a healthy weight? If you are a "volume" eater, choose vegetables and some extra protein (poultry, fish, lean beef) when you feel you need to have more.

Food Item	Standard Portion	Calories in Standard Portion	Large Portion	Calories in Large Portion	Extra Calories from Larger Portion	How long you will need to exercise to burn the extra calories **		
						Walking	Bicycling	Light Jog
Bagel	3-in. dia.	190	4½-in. dia.	360	170	57 min.	19 min.	24 min.
McDonald's fast-food hamburger	3.5 oz.	260	7.5 oz. (Big Mac)	550	290	1 hr. 37 min.	32 min.	41 min.
French fries (average all fast-food)	Small—3 oz.	267	Large—6 oz.	534	267	1 hr. 29 min.	30 min.	38 min.
Soda	6.5 oz.	78	20 oz.	240	162	54 min.	18 min.	23 min.
Subway turkey sandwich (with mayo, and cheese)	6-in.	440	12-in. sub	890	450	2 hrs. 50 min.	50 min.	1 hr 7 min.
Coffee	8-oz. coffee w/ 2 T half and half	45	16-oz. mocha (whole milk and whipped cream)	370	325	1 hr. 48 min.	36 min.	46 min.
Chicken cesar salad (Panera Bread)	6.6 oz. (side salad)	265	13.2 oz.	530	265	1 hr. 28 min.	29 min.	38 min.
Blueberry muffin	Small 2 oz. (home-made)	183	Large 5.8 oz. (Costco bakery)	610	427	2 hr. 22 min.	47 min.	1 hr 1 min.
Rice	4 oz.	103	12 oz.	308	205	1 hr. 8 min.	23 min.	29 min.
Spaghetti and 3 meatballs (home-made)	16 oz.	595	24 oz.	893	298	1 hr. 39 min.	33 min.	43 min.
Pepperoni pizza with thick crust (Domino's)	2 medium slices	430	2 large slices	600	170	57 min.	19 min.	24 min.
Cheesecake	1 slice—3 oz.	273	1 large slice—7 oz.	637	364	1 hr. 21 min.	40 min.	52 min.
Chocolate chip cookie	Chips Ahoy, small, 0.5 oz.	50	Bakery, large, 1.5 oz.	210	160	53 min.	18 min.	23 min.

**Based on a 150-lb. person walking at a moderate speed (3 mph), bicycling at a moderate pace (12-14 mph), lightly jogging

What Does It Take to Lose Weight and Keep It Off?

The National Weight Control Registry (NWCR) is the largest prospective investigation of long-term successful weight loss tracking over 10,000 individuals who have lost significant amounts of weight and kept it off for long periods of time. Here are a few statistics from the Web site:

- 45% of registry participants lost the weight on their own.
- 55% lost weight with the help of some type of program.

- 98% report that they modified their food intake in some way to lose weight.
- 94% increased their physical activity, with the most frequently reported form of activity being walking.
- 78% eat breakfast every day.
- 75% weigh themselves at least once a week.
- 62% watch less than 10 hours of TV per week.
- 90% exercise, on average, about 1 hour per day.

1 Breakfast

In this section you will find some heartier options, some more-traditional options, and some lighter fare. Experiment. See how you feel later in the day when you eat a substantial breakfast or one a bit more well rounded than you may usually eat. See what happens if you eat, say, a higher-protein breakfast. As you will discover, breakfast eaters win out over breakfast skippers in so many ways.

20 Grilled Turkey Chorizo Chilaquiles, Chef Jeff Mora

22 Grilled Apple Stuffed with Oatmeal

23 Grill-Top Vegetable Frittata

24 Salmon "Eggs Benedict" over Sweet Potato Latkes

26 Grilled Fruit over Yogurt

27 Grilled Steak and Eggs

28 Grilled Peanut-Butter-and-Banana Sandwiches

29 Grill-Top Baked Eggs with Salsa

30 Scrambled Tofu with Potato, Lentil, and Sweet Onion Hash

32 Grilled Breakfast Pizza

TOP TEN BENEFITS OF EATING BREAKFAST

- Lower BMI (See above right.)
- Better body composition
- Better blood sugar control
- Less cortisol production
- Better ability to concentrate
- Better ability to problem-solve
- Better mood
- Lower calorie intake overall for the day
- Better nutrient intake
- Better appetite management

Why Bother with Breakfast?

Breakfast may not be the first meal you think of when you think of grilling . . . but I hope it is in when you are trying to lose or maintain your weight. The science is clear: breakfast eaters have a lower body-mass index (BMI) than breakfast skippers. Overweight and obese individuals are more likely to skip breakfast or eat fewer calories at breakfast than trimmer counterparts. Even in those with relatively stable body weight, body composition is better when they consume food at more-regular intervals throughout the day.

More-frequent eating (smaller amounts) is associated with lower fasting serum lipid levels, lower fasting serum concentrations of total cholesterol levels, low-density lipoprotein, decreased mean serum insulin level, and lower mean 24-hour urinary cortical levels. Skipping breakfast is associated with an increased risk of developing metabolic syndrome in adults.

Studies that look at selected indicator nutrients found that breakfast eaters have a better overall intake of nutrients than those who rarely eat breakfast. Women who eat a more-energy-dense breakfast (more calories, within reason of course) tend to eat less overall for the entire day. Men, on the other hand, may need to be more mindful about their breakfast choices and eat a more moderate amount of calories at breakfast to keep in line with total caloric needs. Eating breakfast helps with problem-solving skills, mood, and concentration in school or at work.

What Makes a Good Breakfast?

When you eat one plain bagel (Dunkin Donuts), you have consumed 320 calories and 63 grams of carbohydrate, the equivalent of eating four slices of white bread, with no other nutrients to nourish you. No protein, no vitamin C, no calcium . . . . Grab a granola bar, and it may have many fewer calories (80), but there are still too few nutrients because only one food group, starch, is represented. The ideal breakfast will include some starch but also dairy and/or protein and some fruit for healthy phytonutrients, vitamins, and minerals. Add some healthy fat, too. That breakfast will help your feeling of satiety; you will eat more moderately at every other meal; and it will even help keep your immune system humming along.

How many calories should you shoot for? That is variable. Do you exercise in the morning? Do you wake hungry? Do you have an appetite first thing in the morning? Even on a low-calorie diet, a 300- to 500-calorie start to the day is the right start to the day.

NUTRITION 4-1-1: EGG SENSE

When choosing egg whites for a meal, throw in a whole egg; the yolk contains lutein, which is beneficial for eye health, and lecithin, a natural cholesterol buster. The choline in egg yolk may reduce inflammation markers such as C-reactive protein (CRP) and homocysteine.

Owner of Chef Jeff LLC and Chef Partner in Sam Choy's Pineapple Express, Chef Jeff Mora is the former Chef for the World Champion Los Angeles Lakers and a devoted Environmentalist. His colorful and extensive career began more than 20 years ago at the Century Plaza Hotel under Master Chef Raimund Hofmeister. Since that time, he has worked as a chef in more than 20 countries and served as a member of the U.S. Culinary Olympic Team in 1992 and 1996. His distinction as a chef is in the development of unique menus featuring sustainable meats, seafood, and produce. Chef Jeff serves as a board member for several environmental groups, including the Earth Communications Office, Ocean Futures Society, and The National Marine Sanctuary Foundation.

Personal Wellness: Exercise is important: I spend time hiking and walking with my two large dogs, Pebbles and Bam Bam, a Newfoundland and a Leonburger. My wife and I try to take them for at least 2 walks a day (2–3 miles). We go to the park every morning at 6 AM, and then later in the day we try to take them on the hiking trails in the Santa Monica Mountains above our home.

Nutrition Facts
(1 serving)

Calories	270
Total Fiber	6g
Total Fat	8g
Total Carbs	23g
Total Protein	27g
Vitamin A	20%
Vitamin C	4%
Calcium	15%
Iron	20%

This is a complete meal—carbs, protein, and fat—plus calcium, vitamin A, and iron. Add some sliced mango to boost the vitamin C, and enjoy every bite!

GRILLED TURKEY CHORIZO CHILAQUILES

TURKEY CHORIZO

1 pound ground turkey

1 tablespoon chili powder

1 teaspoon Spanish paprika

½ teaspoon ground coriander

¼ teaspoon ground cumin

¼ teaspoon ground oregano

2 tablespoons red wine vinegar

¼ teaspoon ground black pepper

1 teaspoon salt

2 cloves garlic minced

CHILAQUILES

4 ounces corn tortilla chips

2 cups salsa (your favorite brand)

1 onion, diced

½ cup chopped cilantro

8 egg whites

¼ cup cheddar cheese

1 teaspoon olive oil

Combine all of the turkey chorizo seasonings in a bowl; add the ground turkey; and mix well to combine. Divide the mixture into four equal portions, and form into hamburger-shape patties.

Preheat one side of grill to medium high. Once the grill is hot, cook the turkey chorizo patties about 4 minutes on each side or until cooked to your liking.

While the patties are grilling, add the olive oil to a large sauté pan, and heat it over high heat on the other side. Add the onions, and cook for 2 minutes; add the tortilla chips, and cook for 1 minute; add the salsa, and simmer for 3 minutes; add the eggs, and stir for 2 minutes; add the cheese, and cook for 1 minute.

Toss in ¼ cup of cilantro; divide the mixture into four portions; and place them on four plates. Top each with a turkey chorizo patty, and sprinkle with the remaining cilantro. Serve right away. ❈

4 Servings • Prep: 10 min. • Grill: 20–25 min.

GRILLED APPLE STUFFED WITH OATMEAL

4 apples (McIntosh, Fuji, or Golden Delicious)
½ cup oatmeal, plain (instant)
1½ cups water
½ banana (very ripe, pureed)
1 teaspoon ground cinnamon
⅛ teaspoon ground nutmeg
⅛ teaspoon ground cloves
1 teaspoon vanilla extract
8 walnuts, coarsely ground
1 tablespoon light brown sugar
1–2 lemon slices

Begin by cooking the oatmeal on your stove (medium-high heat). Bring the water to a boil; stir in the oatmeal; add the banana, cinnamon, nutmeg, cloves, vanilla, light brown sugar, and walnuts. Cook for 1 minute, stirring regularly. Cover, and remove from heat.

Trim a thin slice off of the bottom of each apple (keeping it level). Cut off the top of the apple, and using a small paring knife, hollow out the apple to create a cavity for the oatmeal filling.

Preheat one side of grill to medium. Rub the cut parts of the apples with a lemon slice (to keep from browning). Stuff the apples with oatmeal filling; place them on the grill over indirect heat; and close the grill. (The apples will cook more evenly.) Cook for 20–25 minutes. ❋

Nutrition Facts (1 serving = 1 stuffed apple)	
Calories	190
Total Fiber	6g
Total Fat	3g
Total Carbs	41g
Total Protein	4g
Vitamin A	2%
Vitamin C	15%
Calcium	2%
Iron	6%

Add some yogurt to round out this breakfast and help you feel satisfied until lunch.

4 Servings • Prep: 20 min. • Grill: 8–10 min. • Rest: 3–5 min.

GRILL-TOP VEGETABLE FRITTATA

- **1 pint egg whites or yokeless egg substitute**
- **2 tablespoons olive or canola oil**
- **½ cup parboiled and diced new potato**
- **1 cup julienned red onion**
- **1 cup julienned red bell pepper**
- **1 cup chopped fresh baby spinach (or frozen if unavailable)**
- **½ cup shredded sharp cheddar cheese**
- **Salt and pepper to taste**

There are some nutrient-packed vegetables in this breakfast. If you want, add a slice of whole-grain bread.

Preheat grill to high. Place a seasoned 9- to 12-inch cast-iron pan atop the heat. Once the pan is heated, add the oil and potatoes, and cook until crisp, about 3–5 minutes. Add onions and peppers, and soften while stirring.

Reduce heat to low, and add eggs, spinach, cheese, salt, and pepper. Cover the grill, and bake until the egg firms. Let cool for 3–5 minutes; slice into four wedges; and serve straight from the pan. ❈

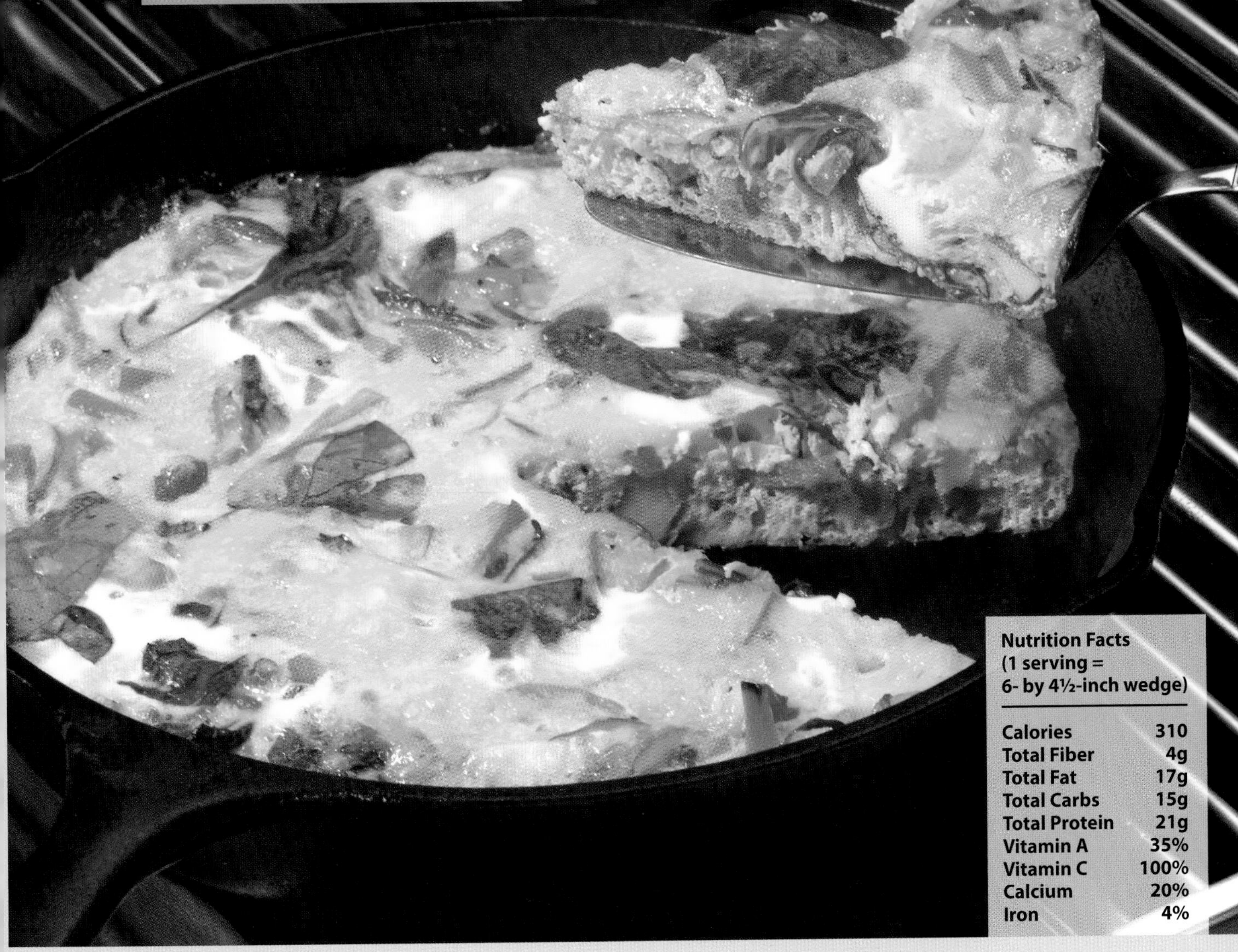

Nutrition Facts (1 serving = 6- by 4½-inch wedge)

Calories	310
Total Fiber	4g
Total Fat	17g
Total Carbs	15g
Total Protein	21g
Vitamin A	35%
Vitamin C	100%
Calcium	20%
Iron	4%

Serve up with a 6-ounce glass of orange juice for a vitamin C punch! DIET MYTH BUSTED: no need to avoid juice; just be mindful of portions. Of course you can always slice and eat an orange instead!

NUTRITION 4-1-1: EXCELLENT EGGS

Save your yolks. The lutein and zeaxanthin responsible for the yolk's yellow pigment have been shown to help prevent macular degeneration. Additionally, eggs are one of the only foods that contains naturally occurring Vitamin D.

SALMON "EGGS BENEDICT" OVER SWEET POTATO LATKES

4 8-ounce salmon fillets, seasoned with salt & pepper (leave skin on; take off before serving)

1 sweet potato, grated

¼ onion, grated

4 eggs

2 egg whites

¼ cup flour

2 scallions

¼ tablespoon salt

¼ tablespoon pepper

2 cups water

1 tablespoon vinegar

HOLLANDAISE SAUCE

⅔ cup plain nonfat Greek yogurt

2 egg yolks

1 tablespoon orange Juice (fresh)

¼ teaspoon orange zest

1 teaspoon dill (fresh)

¼ teaspoon Dijon mustard

¼ teaspoon salt

¼ teaspoon pepper

Begin by making the hollandaise sauce. In a double boiler on your stove, whisk the egg yolks; add the orange juice; and continue whisking. (Egg yolks will become a light pale color when they are cooked, make sure not to let them curdle.) Take the bowl with egg yolks off the stove, and mix in yogurt and the rest of the ingredients for the hollandaise. Set the mixture aside, and begin making potato pancakes.

Place the grated sweet potato and grated onion in a bowl. Add the egg whites (beaten), flour, salt, and pepper. Mix well to combine. Form four pancakes (latkes) with the potato mixture. Place them on a baking sheet, and bake them in an oven at 375°F for 20 minutes.

Preheat grill to medium high. While the latkes are baking, place the seasoned salmon fillets on the grill, and cook until fully done. Right before the salmon is cooked, begin making the poached eggs.

Boil the water in a pot, and add the vinegar. Crack the eggs in a small bowl (individually); add one egg at a time to the boiling water. When the eggs are cooked, take them out of the boiling water using a slotted spoon.

Place a latke on a plate; put a 2-ounce piece of salmon on top of the pancake; top with one poached egg; and drizzle about 1–2 tablespoonfuls of hollandaise sauce over the top. Garnish the dish with dill, and enjoy! ❋

Nutrition Facts (1 serving = 1 latke, 2 ounces salmon, 1 egg, 2 tablespoons sauce)	Calories	240	Vitamin A	35%
	Total Fiber	2g	Vitamin C	10%
	Total Fat	11g	Calcium	8%
	Total Carbs	14g	Iron	8%
	Total Protein	19g		

4 Servings • Prep: 15 min. • Grill: 4–6 min.

GRILLED FRUIT OVER YOGURT

2 bananas, peeled and left whole

¼ pineapple, cut into 1-inch cubes

2 plums, pitted and cut in half lengthwise

8 strawberries, tops cut off, left whole

1 peach, pitted and cut in half lengthwise

4 cups vanilla nonfat Greek yogurt (or your favorite flavor)

Preheat grill to medium high. Grill all of the fruit. (Use skewers if that's easier; remember to soak the skewers in water first to prevent burning.) Take the fruit off of the grill. Cut the bananas and the peaches into four equal pieces. Mix all of the fruit together, and serve over the yogurt. ❊

Nutrition Facts (1 serving = 1 cup yogurt and fruit)

Calories	240
Total Fiber	4g
Total Fat	0.5g
Total Carbs	39g
Total Protein	22g
Vitamin A	6%
Vitamin C	90%
Calcium	15%
Iron	4%

This is a perfect breakfast as is… but you may want to add some nuts for some healthy fat and "sticking" power… or you may want to plan a healthy snack to bridge the gap to lunch. Not everyone likes a hearty breakfast.

GRILLED STEAK AND EGGS

4 3- to 4-ounce beef tenderloin steaks

4 slices turkey bacon

4 shelled eggs

1 bunch asparagus

½ cup diced fresh tomatoes

½ cup julienned red onion,

Spice mixture of salt, pepper, and ground
    fennel seed (for steak) to taste

Salt and pepper to taste

EQUIPMENT NEEDED:

4 pieces aluminum foil (about
10 x 10 inches), lightly oiled

4 or 8 toothpicks

Preheat grill to high. Wrap each steak with a slice of turkey bacon; secure it using a toothpick or two; season with spice mixture; and sear on both sides. Move steaks to a cooler section of the grill to finish.

As the steak cooks, grill the asparagus. Split the grilled asparagus into four portions, and transfer to the four sheets of oiled aluminum foil, already on the grill. Top the asparagus with tomatoes, onions, and one egg per batch, and season to taste. When the eggs and steak are cooked to desired doneness, transfer to a plate and serve. ✵

Great recipe for all those low-carb fans, or add some healthy fruit to get some cancer fighting phytonutrients in!

Nutrition Facts (1 serving = 1 steak and 1 egg)	
Calories	260
Total Fiber	2g
Total Fat	11g
Total Carbs	8g
Total Protein	32g
Vitamin A	20%
Vitamin C	15%
Calcium	6%
Iron	30%

1

BREAKFAST

4 Servings • Prep: 5 min. • Grill: 5 min.

GRILLED PEANUT-BUTTER-AND-BANANA SANDWICHES

8 slices multi-grain bread of your choice

½ cup natural peanut butter

2 large bananas

2 tablespoons clover honey

4 pinches salt

Cooking spray as needed

Preheat one side of grill to low. Make four peanut-butter-and-banana sandwiches by adding 1 tablespoon of peanut butter to each slice of bread. To that add a half banana per sandwich, sliced lengthwise. Drizzle each sandwich with ½ tablespoon of honey and a pinch of salt.

Apply cooking spray as needed to the grill, and place each sandwich at a 45-degree angle to the grates. After 1 or 2 minutes rotate the sandwich 90 degrees. When browned, flip each sandwich and repeat. Serve sliced into triangles. ❋

Add a tall glass of cold milk for added protein (8 more grams) and calcium, and to help wash down this delicious twist on an old-fashioned classic.

Nutrition Facts (1 serving = 1 sandwich)	
Calories	250
Total Fiber	5g
Total Fat	9g
Total Carbs	38g
Total Protein	8g
Vitamin A	0%
Vitamin C	10%
Calcium	4%
Iron	6%

GRILL-TOP BAKED EGGS WITH SALSA

4 zucchinis, cut into thin strips and grilled

2 tablespoons olive oil

8 shelled eggs (or 1 pint egg substitute)

½ cup shredded Gruyère cheese

Salt and pepper to taste

SPECIAL EQUIPMENT NEEDED:

4 8-ounce petite round casserole dishes

Preheat grill to high. Vertically line the walls of the casserole dishes with the pre-grilled zucchini slices, and place them on the grill to preheat. Add ½ tablespoon of oil to the bottom of each dish; then add two eggs or ½ cup of egg substitute. Top with cheese; season with salt and pepper; and cover the grill to bake the eggs.

In a bowl, mix all of the salsa ingredients, and season to taste. When the eggs are mostly firm, remove the dishes from the heat; top with salsa; and serve. ✳

Pair with a cup of berries or melon.

1

BREAKFAST

SALSA

1 cup diced heirloom tomatoes

¼ cup diced red onion

1 tablespoon seeded and diced jalapeño pepper

1 lime, juiced

2 tablespoons chopped cilantro

Salt and pepper to taste

Nutrition Facts (1 serving = 8-ounce petite round casserole dish)	
Calories	290
Total Fiber	5g
Total Fat	19g
Total Carbs	9g
Total Protein	18g
Vitamin A	15%
Vitamin C	35%
Calcium	20%
Iron	15%

SCRAMBLED TOFU WITH POTATO, LENTIL, AND SWEET ONION HASH

POTATO, LENTIL, AND SWEET ONION HASH

½ cup red lentils, cooked

1 tablespoon olive oil

2 cups small-diced onion

¾ cup quartered small red bliss potatoes, cooked

Salt and pepper to taste

1 teaspoon finely chopped fresh thyme

2 tablespoons finely chopped chives

SCRAMBLED TOFU

2 tablespoons olive oil

1 cup small-diced onions

1 cup seeded and small-diced red bell peppers

1 clove garlic, peeled and minced

1 cup medium-diced plum tomatoes

1 pound/pack tofu, firm, diced into ½-in. cubes

2 tablespoons tamari, low-sodium

1 teaspoon turmeric

Salt and pepper to taste

Gather all of the hash ingredients and a large, nonstick sauté pan. Preheat grill to medium high; heat the olive oil in the pan; add the onions; and stir until they begin to brown. Add the potatoes, and without stirring, cook until crispy. Add the lentils; season with salt, pepper, and thyme; and stir. Allow the hash to form a crust on the bottom of the pan.

Now gather all of the scrambled tofu ingredients and a cast-iron pan. Pour the oil into the pan, and sauté the onions, bell peppers, and garlic until tender. Add the tomatoes, tofu, tamari, and turmeric, and bring to a simmer. Season with salt and pepper. Serve the scrambled tofu over the hash. ❋

Lentils are high in iron and fiber and low on the glycemic index. No need to add anything to this complete breakfast.

Nutrition Facts (1 serving)				
	Calories	390	Vitamin A	45%
	Total Fiber	4g	Vitamin C	100%
	Total Fat	22g	Calcium	15%
	Total Carbs	30g	Iron	15%
	Total Protein	17g		

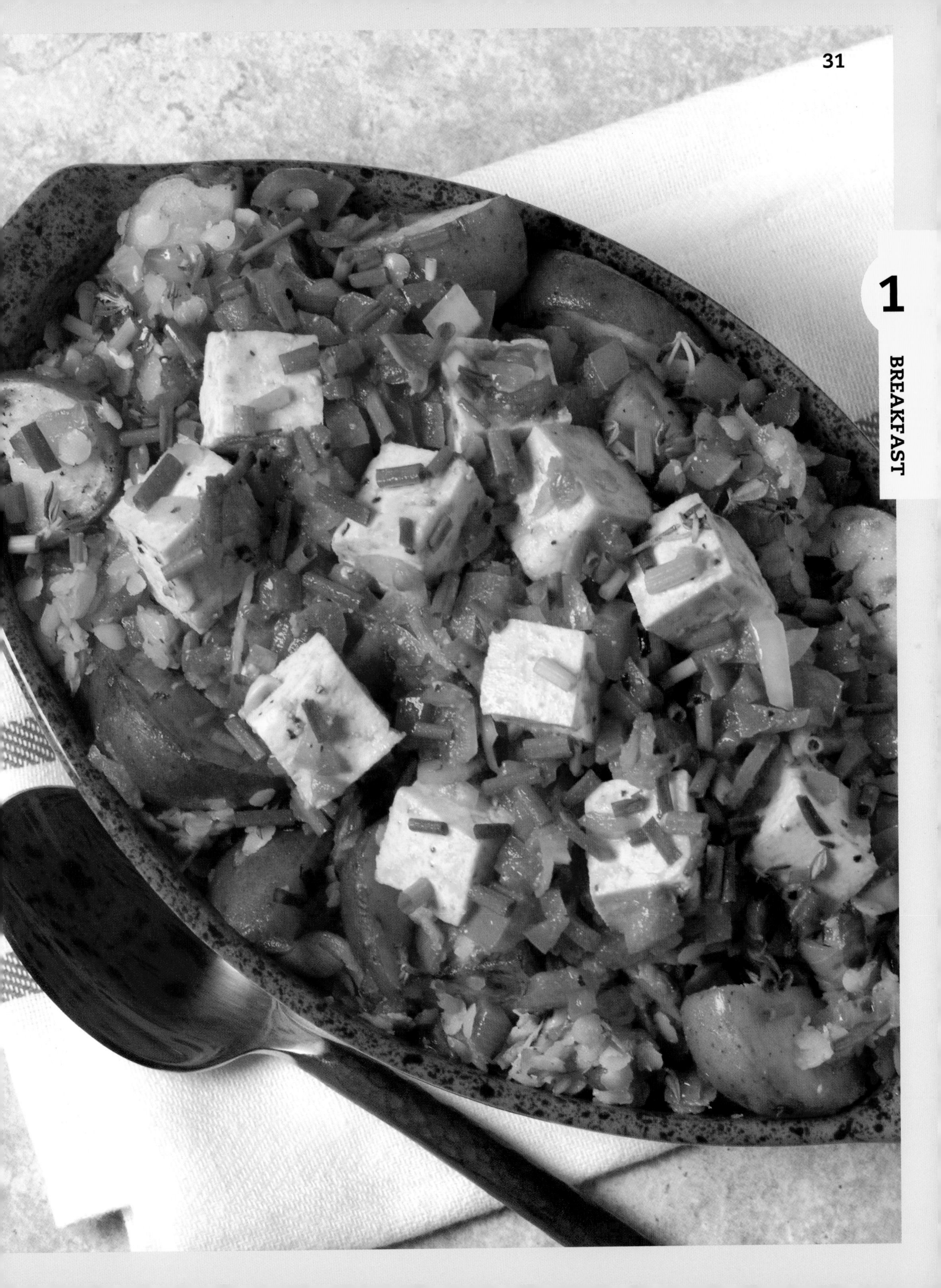

GRILLED BREAKFAST PIZZA

DOUGH (MAKES 2 PIZZAS)

1 teaspoon real maple syrup

1¼ cups warm water

2¼ teaspoons active dry yeast
   (*1 packet / envelope)

1 cup bread flour
   (or all-purpose flour if bread is unavailable)

1½ cups whole-wheat flour

⅔ cup fine-ground cornmeal

1 teaspoon salt

1 tablespoon dry "rubbed" sage

FIXINGS

¼ pound lean breakfast sausage
   (Canadian or turkey bacon optional)

2 tablespoons olive oil (optional)

½ bunch green onion (scallion)

1 cup julienned red bell pepper

2–3 eggs (or 1 cup egg substitute)

½ cup diced tomatoes

½ cup broccoli, steamed soft

2 slices sharp cheddar cheese
   (about 2 ounces)

For the pizza dough, add all dry ingredients together in a mixer. Add syrup and water, and mix on low speed for 10–12 minutes. Set aside, and allow to double in size (30 minutes at room temperature). Punch the air out of the dough; split the batch into two; reshape each portion into a ball; and let it rest, undisturbed, for 15–30 minutes.

Preheat grill to high. Using your hands or a rolling pin, shape the dough on a pan, plate, or peel board, which will allow you to easily transfer the dough to the grill. Carefully place the dough on the grill, and reduce heat to medium low.

Make grill marks on one side of the dough; flip it as soon as marks appear; and top the pizza with the fixings, leaving the egg and cheese for last. Once all of the meat and vegetables are on the pizza, crack the raw eggs on top and cover with the cheese.

Cover the grill, and bake until the eggs are a desired doneness. (If the pizza dough starts to burn, move it to a section of the grill that has been turned off or place it on top of a pizza stone or aluminum foil.) Remove the pizza from the grill; cut it into quarters; and serve. ❀

Note: this recipe will make more dough than that intended to be used; only use 6 ounces of dough per recipe. You can always freeze the remaining dough for another time, or keep it in the refrigerator for 3 days.

Pizza gets a bad rap! In this healthy pizza, you are getting over 100% of your vitamin C for the day. Serve with fruit.

Nutrition Facts (1 serving = 2 ounces, or ¼ pizza)				
	Calories	390	Vitamin A	45%
	Total Fiber	4g	Vitamin C	100%
	Total Fat	22g	Calcium	15%
	Total Carbs	30g	Iron	15%
	Total Protein	17g		

2 Appetizers

Appetizers began in ancient Greece as tiny pre-dinner portions of food to stimulate the appetite for the coming meal. Emphasis: *tiny*.

36 Santa Barbara Prawns with Organic Tequila and Lime Kefir Sauce, Chef Peter Pahk

38 Chicken Satay with Fiery Mango Dipping Sauce

39 Grilled Edamame with Soy-Miso Glaze

40 Grilled-Beet Carpaccio

41 Guacamole-Style Edamame

42 Grilled Crab Cakes

43 Watermelon-and-Feta Skewers

44 Grilled Mushroom Lettuce Wraps

46 Korean-Style Chicken Lettuce Wraps

47 Pepper-and-Garlic Hummus

48 Bruschetta with Apples and Goat Cheese

49 Spinach-Stuffed Artichoke Heart

50 Lettuce Wraps of Grilled Tofu and Moroccan Couscous with Spicy Tomato Chutney

51 Grilled-and-Stuffed Potato Skins

My, how things have changed! In my humble opinion, appetizers have become one of the primary causes of obesity in America (second only to 32-ounce sodas becoming the norm). The popularity of chain-restaurant appetizers, which can contain more calories than entrées, easily alters the way one views appropriate meal size. Most people who eat those appetizers are full before their entrée arrives but feel cheated if they only eat appetizers, so they may go on to overeat. Additionally, the most-popular appetizers are often fried or laden with excessive cheese or meat—or all three.

Here is a "Skinny Tip": skip the appetizer. Or learn to share or to eat only appetizers (like tapas, compliments of Spanish-style eating) for your entire meal. If you like to eat more than just a small amount of appetizer, have a smaller portion of main course, or select the main course based on appetizer selection by balancing calories and macronutrients like carbohydrates and proteins. Want a pasta dish for your entrée? Go with a protein appetizer like a satay or a simple shrimp cocktail. Want steak, fish, or poultry for your meal? Choose a grain-based or vegetable-based appetizer. When dipping, use vegetables instead of chips or bread, which add calories quickly. Choose lean meats in simple sauces. Limit melted cheese to only a sprinkle for that great mouth feel and taste. Do not eat fried food!

It is not just about calories or fat grams; it's about the quality of those calories. Is the fat coming from olives, nuts, avocado, or fish rich in omega 3s rather than land-animal sources? Are the calories from whole grains, which carry nutrient-rich vitamins, minerals, and phytonutrients, or just processed starch?

You don't have to be afraid of appetizers. Just be smart. Enjoy the variety of appetizers that follow, as you won't find any in *Grill Yourself Skinny* that come near the sabotaging levels of these in chain restaurants. Just remember: appetizers are best shared and in small portions, even in your own home. So go on, get grilling!

Typical Chain-Restaurant Appetizers/Calories	
6 Chicken Wings (KFC) with 2 tablespoons of blue cheese dressing	570
Bloomin' Onion (Outback)	1,966
Loaded Potato Skins; 1 plate	2,080
Fried Mozzarella Sticks	537
Classic (12) Nachos w/ beef (Chili's)	1,720
Spinach-Artichoke Dip (Applebee's)	1,565

Source: Calorie King

SANTA BARBARA PRAWNS WITH ORGANIC TEQUILA AND LIME KEFIR SAUCE

Nutrition Facts:
(1 serving = 3 Prawns)

Calories	200
Total Fiber	2g
Total Fat	12g
Total Carbs	12g
Total Protein	7g
Vitamin A	6%
Vitamin C	30%
Calcium	4%
Iron	4%

18 peeled, deveined, Santa Barbara Prawns (or a good wild local shrimp, 16 to a pound)

2 ounces extra-virgin olive oil

1 ounce fresh lemon juice

Sea salt and fresh ground pepper to taste

1 cup "confetti" of red beet

1 cup "confetti" of yellow beet

1 cup "confetti" of cucumber

1½ cups Tequila and Lime Kefir Sauce (See below.)

1 cup chiffonade of romaine lettuce

6 martini glasses

6 sprigs dill

6 sprigs Italian parsley

6 wedges of lime

Preheat grill to medium high. Grill shrimps quickly, about 30 seconds on a side. Season with salt and pepper, olive oil, and lemon juice after grilling. Let cool, about 15 minutes at room temperature.

To make the "confetti" you will need a turning machine. If you don't have one, this garnish is entirely optional.

For the chiffonade of romaine you will need one head of just the heart of the lettuce. Starting from the stem end, repeatedly slice as thin a ribbon of romaine as you can until you have what you need.

To serve, place 1 ounce of romaine at the bottom of a martini glass. Hang a few strands of each kind of "confetti" down the glass. Spoon about 2 ounces of kefir sauce on top of the lettuce and prawns. Garnish with the dill and parsley sprigs and a lime wedge. ♣

TEQUILA-AND-LIME KEFIR SAUCE

14 ounces plain organic kefir

2 ounces organic tequila

Juice of 2 limes (about 1 ounce)

Salt and pepper to taste

An Oahu, HI, native, Chef Peter Pahk is Executive Chef at Xanterra Parks and Resorts' Kingsmill Resort in Williamsburg VA, where he lives with his wife, Patricia. He has been with Xanterra since 1997. Prior to that, Chef Pank was Executive Chef at the Ritz Carlton Hotel Company for 15 years. He traveled extensively abroad to Hong Kong, Bali, Singapore, Korea, Australia, and Mexico as a member of the Ritz Carlton's opening team. Domestically, he helped open hotels in Hawaii, Laguna Niguel, Pasadena, St. Louis, Philadelphia, Aspen, Kansas City, and New Orleans. Chef Pahk is a member of no lees than nine professional organizations, including the American Culinary Federation and the James Beard Foundation. His formal education took place at Syracuse University and the Culinary Institute of America (CIA), in Hyde Park, NY.

Personal wellness: The keys to keeping myself well are keeping mentally healthy, always trying to create a positive work environment when on the job, and not taking work home. I try to follow all of Stephen Covey's seven habits.

CHICKEN SATAY WITH FIERY MANGO DIPPING SAUCE

14 ounces to 1 pound chicken
   breast, cut into strips
8 bamboo skewers
Salt and pepper to taste
Cooking spray as needed

Preheat grill to medium. Weave the bamboo skewers through the chicken strips; season; and grill to an internal temperature of 165°F. In a blender, add all of the other ingredients, and purée until smooth. (You cannot overmix this.) Serve the mango sauce on the side of the grilled chicken. ✦

DIPPING SAUCE
1 orange, juiced
1 lime, juiced
1 mango, ripe, peeled, pitted,
   and rough chopped
1 red jalapeño or Fresno pepper
½ cup roasted and chopped red
   onion
¼ cup fresh cilantro
Salt and pepper to taste

Two or three of these with a side salad or vegetable could also be a meal.

Nutrition Facts:
(1 serving = 2 skewers,
2 ounces each)

Calories	200
Total Fiber	2g
Total Fat	3.5g
Total Carbs	17g
Total Protein	25g
Vitamin A	25%
Vitamin C	60%
Calcium	2%
Iron	2%

GRILLED EDAMAME WITH SOY-MISO GLAZE

16-ounce bag frozen edamame, in their pods

½ cup red, yellow, or white miso Paste

¼ cup sweet mirin (rice wine)

2 tablespoons brown or regular rice vinegar

1 tablespoon Dijon mustard

1 tablespoon minced garlic

1 tablespoon peeled and minced fresh ginger

1 tablespoon toasted sesame seeds

Cooking spray as needed

Preheat grill to medium. In a bowl, mix the miso, mirin, vinegar, mustard, garlic, and ginger. Toss the edamame in the dressing; spray the grill cooking surface; and grill the edamame to desired doneness. Serve immediately, garnished with the toasted sesame seeds. ♣

NUTRITION 4-1-1: EAT MORE EDAMAME

Just ½ cup of edamame has as much fiber as four slices of whole-wheat bread and has as much iron as a 4-ounce piece of chicken. Edamame (or soybean) is in the legume family and is a heart-healthy snack as well as a great addition to soups, salads, and even grains.

Nutrition Facts:
(1 serving =
2.5 ounces of edamame)

Calories	170
Total Fiber	4g
Total Fat	5g
Total Carbs	16g
Total Protein	11g
Vitamin A	10%
Vitamin C	10%
Calcium	6%
Iron	10%

GRILLED-BEET CARPACCIO

2–3 large red beets, skin on
1 cup baby arugula leaves
1 red onion, finely sliced into "wheels"
Cooking spray as needed
1–2 teaspoons tiny capers (optional)
Shaved Parmesan as needed (optional)

Preheat one side of grill to high. Lightly spray the beets with the cooking spray; wrap them in aluminum foil; place them on the cool side of the grill; and cover, cooking them over indirect heat for 45 minutes to 1 hour or until fork tender. Set aside to cool.

In a bowl whisk the olive oil, lemon, and mustard. When the beets are cool, slice as thin as possible and arrange on a plate in a circular, overlapping pattern. Drizzle with the dressing, and garnish with the arugula, onion, capers and shaved Parmesan. ✤

DRESSING
¼ cup extra-virgin olive oil
1 lemon, juiced
1 teaspoon Dijon mustard

A delicious and healthy lower-calorie start to a meal.

Nutrition Facts:
(1 serving = 4–6 ounces)

Calories	70
Total Fiber	2g
Total Fat	3.5g
Total Carbs	9g
Total Protein	2g
Vitamin A	2%
Vitamin C	10%
Calcium	2%
Iron	4%

GUACAMOLE-STYLE EDAMAME

2 limes, quartered

1 cup shelled and defrosted frozen edamame

½ cup roughly chopped cilantro

½ teaspoon freshly ground cumin

2 cloves garlic, minced

¼ red onion, roughly chopped

¼ cup finely chopped red bell pepper

1 pinch cayenne pepper (optional)

Water as needed

Salt and pepper to taste

Preheat grill to high. Place the limes on the grill until lightly charred; remove them; and let them cool. In a food processor, add edamame, cilantro, cumin, garlic, onions, peppers, and cayenne (if desired); squeeze juice from the grilled limes into the mixture; and pulse until you achieve the desired texture. If needed, add small amounts of water to smooth out the texture. Season with salt and pepper, and serve with your favorite vegetables as a dip. ✦

2

APPETIZERS

Try using crudités instead of pita or bread with this dip to enhance the nutrient punch and save calories for other meal options.

Nutrition Facts: (1 serving = 1/3 to ½ cup)

Calories	70
Total Fiber	3g
Total Fat	2g
Total Carbs	9g
Total Protein	5g
Vitamin A	10%
Vitamin C	40%
Calcium	2%
Iron	8%

GRILLED CRAB CAKES

½ pound lump crab meat, picked through for shells

1 red bell pepper, finely diced

4 shallots (or ½ red onion), finely diced

½ cup chopped fresh parsley

¼ cup chopped fresh spearmint

2 garlic cloves

2 tablespoons low-fat mayonnaise

1 tablespoon Dijon mustard

½ teaspoon paprika

Salt and pepper to taste

Instant whole-wheat couscous, ground in a food processor, as needed

Cooking spray as needed

Preheat grill to medium. In a large bowl, mix all ingredients except for couscous and the cooking spray. Adjust seasoning. (Remember that the crab is cooked, so it should be safe to eat.) If you are unable to make sturdy crab cakes from the mixture, add small amounts of the ground couscous until the mixture comes together.

Place a piece of aluminum foil on the grill, and spray with the cooking spray. Place the crab cakes on the aluminum foil, and cook until browned. Flip, and brown the other side. Serve the cakes by themselves or on top of your favorite salad greens. ❧

Though this recipe is an appetizer, you really could have two with a salad or vegetable and call it a meal.

Nutrition Facts:
(1 serving = 4–6 ounces)

Calories	130
Total Fiber	2g
Total Fat	3g
Total Carbs	13g
Total Protein	13g
Vitamin A	40%
Vitamin C	90%
Calcium	8%
Iron	10%

WATERMELON-AND-FETA SKEWERS

½ fresh Watermelon, cut into 1½- x 1½- x 5-inch blocks

1 lime, juiced

Salt and pepper to taste

Cooking spray as needed

4 bamboo skewers, soaked in water

FETA CHEESE MIX

½ cup feta cheese

½ cup peeled and finely diced cucumber

¼ cup thinly sliced fresh spearmint leaves

1 tablespoon rice or champagne vinegar

Salt and pepper to taste

Preheat grill to medium. Place a presoaked skewer into the end of the watermelon; drizzle with lime, salt, and pepper; and spray with cooking spray. Grill to desired doneness.

In a bowl mix the cheese, cucumber, mint, and vinegar; then season. To serve, place one piece of watermelon on a plate and top with spoonful of the cheese mix. ✦

A bit high in calories, this dish begs to be shared or integrated thoughtfully into the rest of your meal.

2

APPETIZERS

NUTRITION 4-1-1: FETA FIGHTS!

Fight food poisoning with feta! Research indicates that lactic acid bacteria in raw sheep's milk feta may naturally neutralize food-poisoning-causing bacteria like *Listeria*.

Nutrition Facts: (1 serving = 1 watermelon segment)	
Calories	250
Total Fiber	3g
Total Fat	7g
Total Carbs	45g
Total Protein	9g
Vitamin A	80%
Vitamin C	90%
Calcium	15%
Iron	10%

GRILLED MUSHROOM LETTUCE WRAPS

14 shitake mushrooms

2 portobello mushrooms (large)

½ red pepper

4 ounces water chestnuts, chopped in chunks

6 cloves garlic, chopped in chunks

1 tablespoon oyster sauce

1 tablespoon fish sauce

1 tablespoon agave

2 tablespoons basil (fresh about 6–8 leaves), sliced in ribbons

12 Boston Bibb lettuce leaves

Cooking spray

Preheat grill to medium high. Grill the mushrooms and pepper until cooked, and take them off grill. Slice the shitake mushrooms and the peppers into strips. Dice the portobello mushrooms into ½-inch pieces.

Place a pan on the grill. (Make sure to spray the pan with cooking spray away from the grill.) Sauté the garlic and water chestnuts, and add agave, fish sauce, oyster sauce, and basil.

Place the mixture into a bowl, and mix with the mushrooms. Arrange the lettuce on a plate, and fill each leaf with the mushroom mixture. Garnish with some thin strips of red pepper. ✤

NUTRITION 4-1-1: MEDICINAL MUSHROOMS

Due to the compound lentinan found in shiitake mushrooms, science has confirmed that this wondrous food can help fight infection and stimulate the immune system. People in China and Japan have used shitake mushrooms for centuries to treat colds and flu.

If you are a "volume" eater and tend to eat as long as there is food around, this is the appetizer for you. Six could keep you busy; yet you will only be at 160 calories (the equivalent of one fried eggroll).

Nutrition Facts:
(1 serving =
3 lettuce wraps)

Calories	80
Total Fiber	4g
Total Fat	0.5g
Total Carbs	17g
Total Protein	4g
Vitamin A	30%
Vitamin C	35%
Calcium	2%
Iron	6%

4 Servings • Prep: 15–20 min. • Marinate: 1 hour
• Grill: 20–25 min., including pineapple (until internal temp. of chicken is 165°F) • Rest: 5 min.

KOREAN-STYLE CHICKEN LETTUCE WRAPS

4 chicken thighs without skin, can also use breast

2 scallions

½ bag shredded cabbage (Cole slaw mix)

12 Boston Bibb lettuce leaves

1 small can sliced pineapples

MARINADE FOR CHICKEN

2 tablespoons low-sodium soy sauce

½ cup pineapple juice reserved from
  canned pineapples above

1 tablespoon toasted sesame oil

SAUCE FOR KIMCHI-STYLE CABBAGE

½ teaspoon siracha hot sauce

2 teaspoons chili garlic sauce

2 tablespoons mirin rice wine vinegar

1 teaspoon fresh ginger

1 teaspoon finely chopped garlic

1 tablespoon fish sauce

Mix the marinade ingredients in a bowl; place the chicken in the marinade; and marinate for at least 1 hour. Preheat grill to high. Take the chicken out of the marinade, and grill it to at least 165°F internal temperature (about 15–20 minutes).

While the chicken is cooking, mix all of the ingredients for the kimchi sauce together. Toss in the cabbage, making sure to coat well.

Once the chicken is cooked, take it off the grill and let it rest for 5 minutes. Grill the pineapple slices to use as a garnish. Slice the chicken into strips; arrange the lettuce on a plate; and place chicken in each leaf (about one chicken thigh sliced for 3 lettuce leaves).

Top chicken with kimchi cabbage. Cut the grilled pineapple slices in half, and garnish each wrap with ½ slice. ♣

Serving size says three, but you can have just one for 63 calories and leave room to taste other appetizers or move on to the meal.

Nutrition Facts:
(1 serving = 3 wraps)

Calories	190
Total Fiber	1g
Total Fat	7g
Total Carbs	17g
Total Protein	16g
Vitamin A	30%
Vitamin C	35%
Calcium	4%
Iron	10%

PEPPER-AND-GARLIC HUMMUS

1 red bell pepper

2 cloves garlic, lightly oiled and wrapped in aluminum foil

1 15-ounce can of garbanzo beans, drained

¼ cup tahini

1 tablespoon extra-virgin olive oil

1 lemon, juiced

Salt and pepper to taste

Whole-grain crackers or vegetables (to dip) as needed

Often hummus is paired with pita or even pretzels, but try an assortment of vegetables instead to save calories and to get in those valuable nutrients.

Preheat grill to high. Place both the aluminum-wrapped garlic and pepper on the grill. Char the outside of the pepper until black. Cook the garlic to the desired roasted amount.

Place the pepper in a paper bag or covered bowl, and let it cool until comfortable to handle. Remove the blacked skin, seeds, and stem from the pepper. In a food processor, blend all other ingredients with the pepper and garlic. Serve with your favorite whole-grain cracker or vegetables. ♣

Note: if the mixture is thicker than you desire, just thin it out with water.

2

APPETIZERS

NUTRITION 4-1-1: HEALTHY HUMMUS

This versatile spread combines garbanzo beans with tahini (sesame paste) to provide a healthy dose of folic acid, zinc, magnesium, calcium, and iron.

Nutrition Facts:
(1 serving = ¼ cup)

Calories	120
Total Fiber	3g
Total Fat	7g
Total Carbs	11g
Total Protein	4g
Vitamin A	10%
Vitamin C	40%
Calcium	4%
Iron	6%

BRUSCHETTA WITH APPLES AND GOAT CHEESE

16–18 Belgium endive leaves (yellow or white) OR
8 whole-wheat ciabatta bread slices, ¾–1 inch thick
Olive oil as needed

BRUSCHETTA

6 plum tomatoes, diced
2 Granny Smith or other firm apple, diced
½ yellow onion, diced
1 tablespoon olive oil
¼ cup basil, rolled and cut into strips
2 tablespoons balsamic vinegar
Salt and pepper to taste

GARNISH

4 ounces chèvre (goat cheese)
¼ cup chopped fresh Italian parsley
½ cup toasted and chopped pecans (optional)

In a bowl, mix the tomatoes, apple, onion, basil, oil, and vinegar. Season, and set aside.

Preheat grill to high. Lightly brush the endive leaves with oil, and grill them to desired doneness (or leave them raw as shown). If you're using bread slices instead, follow this step, making them pretty crisp and firm.

Serve the tomato and apple mixture atop the endive leaves or toasted slices of bread, and garnish with crumbles of the cheese, parsley, and chopped nuts. ✤

Nutrition Facts: (1 serving = 2 endive leaves)	
Calories	170
Total Fiber	4g
Total Fat	13g
Total Carbs	11g
Total Protein	4g
Vitamin A	15%
Vitamin C	20%
Calcium	4%
Iron	6%

Nutrition Facts: (1 serving = 1 bread slice)	
Calories	290
Total Fiber	4g
Total Fat	15g
Total Carbs	34g
Total Protein	8g
Vitamin A	15%
Vitamin C	20%
Calcium	4%
Iron	4%

NUTRITION 4-1-1: LACTOSE-FREE GOAT CHEESE

Think you can't stomach dairy? Give goat cheese a chance. Goat cheese does not have any lactose in it, so people who can't tolerate cow's milk are able to consume goat's milk without any ill effects.

SPINACH-STUFFED ARTICHOKE HEARTS

4 large artichokes
¼ cup balsamic vinegar
½ cup brown rice vinegar
¼ cup water
1 tablespoon minced ginger
2 tablespoons olive oil
Salt and pepper to taste

STUFFING
4–6 ounces low-fat cottage cheese
1½ cups chopped frozen or baby spinach
2–4 tablespoons dry vegetable soup mix
1 tablespoon finely diced red onion
1 teaspoon lemon juice
Salt and pepper to taste

Slice off the artichoke tops, and trim the stems using a paring knife. Boil the artichokes in water until the bottoms become fork tender or the petals start to pull off easily. Drain and cool.

Cut each artichoke in half, tip to tip, and using a spoon, remove the "hair like" center and any purple petals. In a bowl, mix the vinegars, water, ginger, oil, salt, and pepper. Toss in the cool artichokes, and let marinate for up to 12 hours.

For the stuffing, add the cottage cheese, spinach, soup mix, onion, and lemon juice. Season, and set aside in the refrigerator for up to 2 days.

Preheat grill to high. Drain the artichokes, and place the cut side down on the grill. Cook until lightly browned. Flip, and place a dollop of the spinach mix on top of the artichoke. Turn off one side of the grill; lower the cover; and grill the stuffed artichoke over indirect heat until the mixture starts to brown. Remove, and serve hot or at room temperature. ♣

2

APPETIZERS

NUTRITION 4-1-1: HEALING ARTICHOKE
Artichokes contain the flavonoid (plant pigment) silymarin, which supports healthy liver function. Adding grilled artichoke hearts to a salad is a delicious way to boost your natural healing system.

Nutrition Facts:
(1 serving =
½ stuffed artichoke)

Calories	130
Total Fiber	5g
Total Fat	4.5g
Total Carbs	17g
Total Protein	6g
Vitamin A	30%
Vitamin C	20%
Calcium	10%
Iron	8%

LETTUCE WRAPS OF GRILLED TOFU AND MOROCCAN COUSCOUS WITH SPICY TOMATO CHUTNEY

½ package or 8 ounces extra-firm tofu, sliced into 1-inch-thick slices

12 Boston Bibb lettuce leaves

Salt and pepper to taste

COUSCOUS

¼ cup whole-wheat couscous

¼ cup 100-percent apple juice

Pinch salt

⅛ teaspoon cinnamon

⅛ teaspoon cumin

Pinch coriander

1 tablespoon fresh orange juice

2 fresh apricots, cut in half and grilled

1 tablespoon raisins

SPICY TOMATO CHUTNEY

½ pint grape tomatoes

3 cloves garlic

⅛ habanero pepper (very spicy pepper, be sure to keep wear gloves when chopping, and only use a very little)

½ onion

1 teaspoon chili powder

½ teaspoon curry powder

½ teaspoon ginger powder

Preheat grill to medium high. Before putting tofu on grill, make sure to squeeze out excess water, and pat dry with a paper towel. Season tofu with salt and pepper, and grill it and the apricots on both sides. Take the tofu and apricots off of the grill, and set them aside.

Cook the couscous in apple juice. Dice the grilled apricots, and add them and all other ingredients to the couscous. When the couscous is done, fluff it with a fork.

To make the tomato chutney, place a pot on the grill. Sauté the tomatoes and onions until they're very soft. Add in the rest of the ingredients for chutney, and cook for 20 minutes until a chutney consistency is formed. Arrange lettuce on a plate; add 2 tablespoons of couscous into lettuce; then top with tofu. Add tomato chutney last. ♣

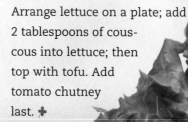

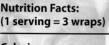

Nutrition Facts: (1 serving = 3 wraps)	
Calories	150
Total Fiber	4g
Total Fat	4g
Total Carbs	21g
Total Protein	10g
Vitamin A	10%
Vitamin C	25%
Calcium	10%
Iron	15%

GRILLED-AND-STUFFED POTATO SKINS

4 large red bliss potatoes

Cooking spray as needed

Salt as needed

STUFFING

½ cup sliced yellow summer squash

½ cup sliced zucchini

½ large red bell pepper, julienned

½ large green pablano pepper, julienned

1 small red onion, julienned

1 tablespoon olive oil

¼ cup balsamic vinegar

Salt and pepper to taste

¼ cup finely chopped parsley

¼ cup Parmesan cheese (optional)

Preheat one side of grill to high. Spray the potatoes with cooking spray; lightly coat with salt; and wrap in aluminum foil. Using indirect heat, cook the potatoes on the grill for 30 minutes or until fork tender.

For the stuffing, mix all of the vegetables, oil, vinegar, salt, and pepper in a bowl. Using a perforated grill basket, sauté the vegetables on the grill until al dente. Slice the potatoes in half; hollow the skins with a spoon; and stuff with the sautéed vegetables. (Optionally, you can top the stuffed potatoes with the cheese and return to the grill to melt.)

Serve on a plate, topped with the chopped parsley. ✦

2

APPETIZERS

NUTRITION 4-1-1: BEST POTATO FOR YOU?

Sweet potatoes are loaded with vitamin C, potassium, and fiber, making them of the best foods you can eat—skin and all. Is purple more your color? Research shows that eating purple potatoes daily can significantly lower blood pressure.

Nutrition Facts:
(1 serving =
½ stuffed potato)

Calories	120
Total Fiber	3g
Total Fat	3g
Total Carbs	21g
Total Protein	4g
Vitamin A	15%
Vitamin C	40%
Calcium	6%
Iron	6%

3 Salads

Salad ...you just feel healthier ordering one ...and for good reason! Consuming a plant-based (not necessarily plant only) diet has been shown time and again to reduce the risk for heart disease and heart attacks, stroke, and diabetes. Certain vegetables may offer protection against some types of cancers. The array of vitamins, minerals, and phytonutrients in all plant-based foods helps keep our eyes healthy, our skin supple, and our arteries pumping blood at just the right rate. The fiber and water content of vegetables certainly help anyone trying to lose weight. But when we dress them up, they can be a dieter's nightmare.

54 Moroccan Grilled-Fennel Salad, Chef Brad Farmerie

56 Tomato, Chickpea, and Onion Salad with Grilled-Lemon Vinaigrette

57 Grilled-Beet Salad with Balsamic Pesto

58 Warm Flank Steak, Tomato, and Asparagus Salad

59 Grilled Sardines over Greek Salad

60 Fennel, Clementine, and Grilled-Ricotta-Salata Salad

61 Healthy Caesar Salad with Grilled Romaine

62 Garden Veggie Antipasto

64 Grilled-Watermelon and Watercress Salad

65 Tossed Mushrooms and Baby Spinach

66 Seared-Radicchio Salad with Mustard Vinaigrette

67 Grilled-Corn and Tomato Salad

How To Build a Healthy Salad

Loading high-fat meats, cheeses, croutons, and mayonnaise-laden toppings of low nutritional value on lettuce will not make for a healthy meal. Instead, start with a base of colorful lettuce or chopped vegetables, and then (depending on whether it's your main entrée or a side dish) add lean meats, more nutrient-rich vegetables, some beans, grains, nuts, or even fruit. Lastly, toss with a delicious yet healthy olive-oil-based dressing—in fact, the oil may help you absorb some of the fat-soluble nutrients in the vegetables.

Not all salads start with a green leafy foundation. Some are protein based (grilled flank steak), predominately starch based (potato or corn salad), or vegetable based (beet salad) and are meant to be a starter or side dish or rounded out as part of a complete meal.

Because there is no fat in vegetables, most of the fat in the *Grill Yourself Skinny* salads come from healthful sources like olive or olive oils, nuts, or avocado. Still, you must choose your portions wisely, depending whether the salad is intended as a main course or as a side dish. If the salad is your entrée, for example, ensure that it has adequate protein (15–21 grams). If it doesn't, add some grilled chicken, fish, beef, or tofu on top—or choose a protein-rich appetizer as a pairing.

The U.S. Department of Agriculture's MyPlate.gov recommends that one-half of your meal plate be fruits and vegetables. The recipes that follow help you rise to that challenge.

Just because a dish is a salad doesn't mean it is good for you. For example:

UNHEALTHY SALAD:
2 cups Iceberg lettuce
½ cup shredded cheddar cheese
½ cup bacon pieces
½ cup croutons
2 tablespoons ranch dressing

643 cal, 50g fat (mostly saturated), 30g protein
RDA%: 18% vit A, 3% vit C, 39% calcium (from sources high in saturated fat), 25% iron

Compare that salad to any of the *Grill Yourself Skinny* salads. The Grilled Sardines over Greek Salad (page 59), for example, is packed with nutrient-rich vegetables like red peppers and tomatoes, has some feta cheese and sardines for protein, and uses olive oil, lemon, oregano, salt, and pepper as a dressing. At 360 calories a serving, it has almost half the calories of the sample salad yet provides adequate protein at half the fat (and healthy fat at that), 21g protein, 25g fat, plus much more vitamin A and C (at 300% and 100%, respectively). It is a far greater nutritional powerhouse of a salad compared with the example above.

As Executive Chef for AvroKO Hospitality Group, Brad Farmerie has helped open many high-profile restaurants in NYC: PUBLIC Restaurant, which has been awarded a Michelin star every year since 2009; The Daily, a small plate and cocktail-focused concept with a menu that changes daily; Madam Geneva, a gin den; Saxon + Parole, showcasing domestic meat and seafood; and The Thomas and Fagiani's located in Napa, California.

Chef Brad grew up in Pittsburgh, PA, and completed a Grande Diplome at Le Cordon Bleu London. Named a StarChefs' Rising Star Chef and Food Arts' Emerging Tastemaker, Brad is listed among Global Magazine's Top 50 Chefs to Watch.

Personal Wellness: I'm pretty serious about feeding my family delicious, nutritious meals. An abundance of seasonal veggies get juiced, pickled, roasted, and grilled to provide different flavors and textures and are incorporated into many parts of any dish and every meal, keeping the kids nourished without making them eat a sad salad or some uninspired pile of veggies served up as an afterthought to the main course offering. In this way, "wellness" becomes a lifestyle. If vegetables are treated with love and imagination when cooking, they are just as interesting and just as delicious as any animal.

NUTRITION 4-1-1:
FENNEL FOR YOUR ARTERIES
Fennel contains the flavonoid quercetin, which protects the body from free-radical damage and may help reduce the risk of atherosclerosis.

MOROCCAN GRILLED-FENNEL SALAD

Fennel is one of my favorite vegetables, and this is a quick and easy way to prepare it—all of the preparation, including the grilling, can be done in advance. The charred fennel matches nicely with the sweet sun-dried tomatoes, smoky almonds, and salty olives to make a dish that is crunchy, colorful, and deliciously memorable. Serve this salad as a light way to start a meal or as a side dish to lamb, shrimp, or almost anything from the grill. 🌶

3

SALADS

4 fist-sized heads of fennel, each fennel cut into 6 wedges

1 cup orange juice

1½ teaspoons salt

⅔ teaspoon Aleppo chili flakes

2½ teaspoons ground cumin

Zest and juice of 1 lemon

¾ cup extra-virgin olive oil

¼ cup pitted Kalamata olive halves

½ cup sun-dried tomato halves

⅛ cup roughly chopped smoked almonds

¼ cup roughly chopped parsley

2 oranges, cut into segments

2–3 hearts romaine lettuce, chopped into large pieces

¼ cup crumbled feta cheese

Combine the orange juice, salt, chili flakes, cumin, and lemon in a saucepot, and place over medium heat. Bring the mixture to a boil, and continue to cook until the mix has reduced by half. Allow the liquid to cool to room temperature; then add ⅔ cup of olive oil. Place the fennel wedges into a mixing bowl, and pour the liquid over them, stirring to mix thoroughly.

Preheat grill to medium. Grill the marinated fennel until it chars nicely. Do not keep moving the wedges or turn them prematurely, as this will not allow them to get nice, flavorful grill marks on them. When the fennel is cooked (light char on the outside and just starting to soften), remove the wedges from the grill and place them back into the marinade to cool to room temperature. Drain the fennel just before serving, saving the marinade as the salad dressing.

Place the olives, tomatoes, almonds, parsley, oranges, and lettuce into a mixing bowl, and stir them together. Add the fennel; drizzle enough of the fennel marinade to dress the salad; and stir just to combine. Place the salad onto serving plates; sprinkle with the feta cheese; and drizzle the remaining olive oil as you serve the salad. 🌶

Nutrition Facts (1 serving = 2.5 cups)				
	Calories	460	Vitamin A	560%
	Total Fiber	14g	Vitamin C	130%
	Total Fat	34g	Calcium	25%
	Total Carbs	37g	Iron	30%
	Total Protein	10g		

TOMATO, CHICKPEA, AND ONION SALAD WITH GRILLED-LEMON VINAIGRETTE

1 cup medium-diced tomato

1 cup chickpeas (garbanzo beans), rinsed and dried

½ cup thinly sliced red onion

½ cup cleaned and roughly torn fresh basil

Salt and pepper to taste

4 cups salad greens (optional)

VINAIGRETTE

2 tablespoons extra-virgin olive oil

2 lemons, cut in half

1 teaspoon Dijon mustard

1 garlic clove, minced

Salt and pepper to taste

Preheat grill to medium. Grill the lemon halves just until grill marks appear; then squeeze the juice from the seared lemons. Retain the grilled lemons as a garnish. In a bowl, add the oil, one-half of the lemon juice, mustard, garlic, salt, and pepper (Do not add all of the lemon juice, just in case the lemon overpowers the other flavors. Adjust the amount of lemon juice to your taste. If the lemon flavor is too strong, add oil to cut the intensity and discard some of the vinaigrette to limit the amount of fat you add to the recipe.)

Once you like the vinaigrette, add the tomatoes, chickpeas, onions, and basil. Toss to coat. Adjust seasonings, and serve on salad greens or by itself. 🐞

Nutrition Facts: (1 serving = ¾–1 cup)	
Calories	160
Total Fiber	6g
Total Fat	8g
Total Carbs	19g
Total Protein	5g
Vitamin A	50%
Vitamin C	35%
Calcium	8%
Iron	10%

4 Servings • Prep: 10–15 min. • Grill: 10–15 min. • Rest: 15–20 min.

57

GRILLED-BEET SALAD WITH BALSAMIC PESTO

3

SALADS

4 large beets, peeled and cut into quarters

½ cup julienned red onion

1 lemon, quartered lengthwise

Salt and pepper to taste

Cooking spray as needed

BALSAMIC PESTO SAUCE

2 cups sweet Italian basil

¼ cup toasted pine nuts (optional to use other nuts)

2 tablespoons Romano cheese

1 garlic clove, roasted

¼ cup extra-virgin olive oil

¼ cup balsamic vinegar

Salt and pepper to taste

Preheat grill to high. Spray the grill lightly with the cooking spray. Sear the beets on all sides. Turn the grill down to low, and finish cooking the beets until fork tender. Remove them from the grill; season; and let cool. When cool enough to handle, dice the beets into bite-sized chunks.

For the pesto sauce, place all of the ingredients into a food processor. Purée on high until smooth. (If the mixture is too dry, add water as needed.) Add the pesto and julienned onions to the beets, and finish with a squeeze of fresh lemon juice. ❧

Pair this dish with a protein entrée.

Nutrition Facts:
(1 serving = 1 beet,
1 tablespoon pesto)

Calories	70
Total Fiber	3g
Total Fat	3g
Total Carbs	10g
Total Protein	2g
Vitamin A	2%
Vitamin C	8%
Calcium	2%
Iron	4%

WARM FLANK STEAK, TOMATO, AND ASPARAGUS SALAD

1½ pounds flank steak, lean, fat trimmed

1 pint grape tomatoes

1 bunch asparagus

STEAK MARINADE

½ cup soy sauce

¼ cup olive oil

1 tablespoon Dijon mustard

2 cloves garlic

1 tablespoon toasted sesame-seed oil

1 tablespoon agave

1 tablespoon balsamic vinegar

1 teaspoon salt

Black pepper to taste

1 tablespoon fresh thyme

In a one-gallon sealable plastic bag, combine all ingredients for the steak marinade. Put the steak into the bag; seal it; and lay it flat in a refrigerator. (This way, the marinade will evenly cover the entire steak.) Marinate the steak for 1½ hours.

Preheat grill to high. Take the steak out of the marinade. (Keep the marinade for later use as a sauce.) Grill the steak to desired doneness; then let it rest for 10 minutes while covered with aluminum foil. (This will keep the juices in the steak.)

Turn grill down to medium. Grill the tomatoes in a perforated pan until the skin of the tomatoes becomes wrinkled. At the same time, grill the asparagus until grill marks appear, and place a pot on the grill to cook the marinade until it comes to a boil. (This will kill any bacterial from the raw steak.)

Slice the steak against the grain, and cut the asparagus into thirds. Use a salad bowl to toss the steak, asparagus, and tomatoes together in the sauce. Serve the salad warm.

This salad may be served either as a main dish or as a side paired with an appetizer (such as hummus) or starch.

Nutrition Facts: (1 serving = 4 ounces flank steak)

Calories	330
Total Fiber	2g
Total Fat	19g
Total Carbs	12g
Total Protein	29g
Vitamin A	20%
Vitamin C	20%
Calcium	6%
Iron	20%

GRILLED SARDINES OVER GREEK SALAD

12 small sardines, fresh, not from a can (heads and
    tails cut off, seasoned with oil, salt, pepper, and
    red chili pepper flakes)

1 head romaine lettuce, rinsed, dried, and chopped

½ red onion, thinly sliced

1 sweet red pepper, sliced in strips

½ green pepper, sliced in strips

¾ English cucumber, cut in half lengthwise,
    then sliced

⅓ cup crumbled feta cheese

1 tomato, chopped

¼ cup extra-virgin olive oil

¾ teaspoon fresh oregano, chopped

½ lemon, juiced

Salt and pepper to taste

Preheat grill to medium high. Grill sardines on both sides.

In a bowl, whisk together the olive oil, lemon juice, oregano, salt, and pepper. In a large salad bowl, combine the romaine lettuce, feta cheese, cucumber, peppers, onion, and tomato. Pour the dressing over the salad, and toss to coat entire salad evenly. Place sardines over the top of the salad. ❦

This is a great main-dish salad, and it leaves just enough room for either an appetizer, dessert, or glass of wine.

3

SALADS

NUTRITION 4-1-1: OMEGA-RICH SARDINES

Most Americans are deficient in omega-3s, and sardines are a great way to incorporate more of them into your diet.

Nutrition Facts:
(1 serving = 3 sardines, 1 cup salad)

Calories	360
Total Fiber	6g
Total Fat	25g
Total Carbs	14g
Total Protein	21g
Vitamin A	300%
Vitamin C	110%
Calcium	20%
Iron	15%

4 Servings • Prep: 10 min. • Grill: 1–3 min.

FENNEL, CLEMENTINE, AND GRILLED-RICOTTA-SALATA SALAD

4–6 ounces ricotta salata cheese

2 cups shaved fennel, shaved on a mandolin
   (fronds reserved for garnish)

4 clementines, peeled and cut into bite-size sections

½ red onion, julienned

2 tablespoons pine nuts, toasted, or walnuts

¼ cup olive oil

½ lemon, juiced

Salt and pepper to taste

Cooking spray as needed

Preheat grill to high. Spray the ricotta salata cheese lightly with the cooking spray, and sear it on both sides, being careful not to burn it. Let the cheese cool, and dice it into ½-inch pieces.

For the salad, add olive oil and lemon juice together in a bowl, mixing thoroughly. Add the fennel, clementine sections, onion, and pine nuts. Adjust the salt-and-pepper seasoning. Lightly fold in the diced cheese, and serve garnished with the fennel fronds. 🐞

Nutrition Facts:
(1 serving = 1 cup,
1–1½ ounces cheese)

Calories	250
Total Fiber	5g
Total Fat	17g
Total Carbs	18g
Total Protein	5g
Vitamin A	2%
Vitamin C	80%
Calcium	10%
Iron	4%

You can always add more cheese if you're having this as an entrée, or substitute pine nuts with your favorite nuts.

HEALTHY CAESAR SALAD WITH GRILLED ROMAINE

1 head romaine lettuce, clean and quartered

Whole-wheat croutons as needed (optional)

Parmesan cheese, shredded, as needed (optional)

Cooking spray as needed

Salt and pepper to taste

CAESAR DRESSING

½ cup fat-free plain Greek yogurt

1 teaspoon Dijon mustard

2 garlic cloves, roasted

1 teaspoon anchovy paste (optional)

1 tablespoon fresh lemon juice

1 teaspoon rice wine vinegar

2 tablespoons olive oil

1 teaspoon Worcestershire sauce

Salt and pepper to taste

Combine the mustard, garlic, anchovy paste (optional), lemon juice, vinegar, and Worcestershire sauce in a blender, and blend until smooth. Add the oil, and blend until incorporated. Fold this purée into the yogurt, and season to taste with salt and pepper.

Preheat grill to medium. Grill the Romaine lettuce until grill-marked on one side, about 90 seconds, and set aside to cool. Rough-chop the lettuce, and toss it with a small amount (¼ cup or less) of the dressing. Season to taste with salt and pepper, and serve with or without croutons and Parmesan. 🍒

3

SALADS

Turkey Drumstick with Apple-Maple BBQ sauce, page 92

Note: You can save the rest of the dressing for 3–4 days in the refrigerator.

Nutrition Facts:
(1 serving/ ¼ lettuce head, ½ ounce dressing)

Calories	60
Total Fiber	4g
Total Fat	2g
Total Carbs	8g
Total Protein	3g
Vitamin A	270%
Vitamin C	10%
Calcium	6%
Iron	10%

GARDEN VEGGIE ANTIPASTO

2 red or green bell peppers, quartered

2 Japanese eggplants, sliced lengthwise

1 yellow crookneck squash, sliced lengthwise

1 portobello mushroom, stem and "gills" removed

1 fennel bulb, quartered

1 bunch asparagus, trimmed

1 red onion, quartered

Salt and pepper to taste

DRESSING

¼ cup orange juice

1 tablespoon balsamic or rice vinegar

½ teaspoon Dijon mustard

2 tablespoons olive oil

1 teaspoon toasted walnut oil

Salt and pepper to taste

Preheat grill to medium high. Grill all of the prepared vegetables until done, about 5 to 10 minutes. Don't overcook.

In a bowl, mix the juice, vinegar, mustard, oils, salt, and pepper. Arrange the grilled vegetables, whole or rough-chopped, on a platter or individually plated. Lightly drizzle the vegetables with a small amount of the dressing (about 1 teaspoon per serving). Serve hot or at room temperature, with some extra dressing on the side. 🐞

Nutrition Facts:
(1 serving = 1 cup salad,
1 teaspoon dressing)

Calories	140
Total Fiber	9g
Total Fat	5g
Total Carbs	23g
Total Protein	6g
Vitamin A	60%
Vitamin C	170%
Calcium	8%
Iron	20%

4 Servings • Prep: 5 min. • Grill: 6–10 min.

GRILLED-WATERMELON AND WATERCRESS SALAD

4 large watermelon slices

2 bunches (about 2 cups) watercress, rinsed

2 tablespoons olive oil

½ lemon, juiced

Salt and pepper to taste

Cooking spray as needed

You can use this tasty dish as a side salad.

Preheat grill to high. Spray the hottest part of the grill with the cooking spray, and carefully place the melon slices at a 45-degree angle to the grills. Because of the high moisture content, the slices will take several minutes to mark, depending on the heat of your grill. Do not move them until they are done. When one side is marked, flip and repeat on the other side.

In a bowl, mix the oil, lemon juice, and watercress, tossing to coat. Season the coated watercress with salt and pepper, and place on four plates. Top each watercress pile with a slice of the grilled watermelon, and serve. 🍉

Note: Shown "family style."

Nutrition Facts:
(1 serving = 1 watermelon slice, ½ cup watercress)

Calories	150
Total Fiber	1g
Total Fat	7g
Total Carbs	22g
Total Protein	2g
Vitamin A	45%
Vitamin C	60%
Calcium	4%
Iron	4%

NUTRITION 4-1-1: HYDRATING WATERMELON

As its name suggests, watermelon is approximately 92% water, making it a delicious way to contribute to hydration.

TOSSED MUSHROOMS AND BABY SPINACH

3–4 portobello mushrooms, stems and "gills" removed

2 tablespoons apple-cider, balsamic, or sherry vinegar

4 tablespoons extra-virgin olive oil

1 garlic clove, roasted and minced

Salt and pepper to taste

1 small red onion, thinly sliced

½ pound baby spinach

2 tablespoons pine nuts, lightly toasted
     (other nuts optional)

1 hard-boiled egg, finely chopped (optional)

1 ounce crumbled goat cheese (optional)

Preheat grill to medium high. In a metal bowl, combine the vinegar of choice, oil, garlic, salt, pepper, and onion, and leave it on or near the grill to warm up, making sure it doesn't get too hot and burn.

Grill the mushrooms until soft, about 3 to 5 minutes per side. When the mushrooms are done, carefully remove them using a pair of tongs; cut them up while still hot; and add them to the vinaigrette. Immediately add the spinach, and toss the mixture to wilt the spinach. Add the pine nuts, egg, and cheese. Adjust the seasonings, and serve.

3

SALADS

Not high enough in protein to be used as an entrée, this dish is great as a side salad to almost any protein-based entrée or appetizer: fish, meat, or poultry.

Nutrition Facts: (1 serving = 1 cup)	
Calories	270
Total Fiber	7g
Total Fat	19g
Total Carbs	20g
Total Protein	8g
Vitamin A	45%
Vitamin C	15%
Calcium	8%
Iron	15%

4 Servings • Prep: 5–10 min. • Grill: 1–2 min. • Rest: 5–10 min.

SEARED-RADICCHIO SALAD WITH MUSTARD VINAIGRETTE

2 heads radicchio, cleaned and quartered
½ lemon, juiced
1 tablespoon rice wine vinegar
1 tablespoon Dijon mustard
4 tablespoons olive oil, extra-virgin
Salt and pepper to taste
2 tablespoons Parmesan cheese, shredded (optional)

Falling into the category of Mediterranean style, this salad uses olive oil, which adds calories but also healthy fat and taste. Without it, radicchio can be quite bitter and not as appealing to the palate.

Preheat grill to high. In a bowl, mix the lemon juice, vinegar, mustard, oil, salt, and pepper. Toss the radicchio in the dressing, and grill for a minute or two until marked. (Radicchio tends to be bitter, and grill marks add bitterness, so be sure not to grill for too long unless you like the bitter notes.)

Remove the radicchio from the heat, and let it cool to room temperature. Rough-chop the radicchio, and serve it alone or topped with a small amount of Parmesan.

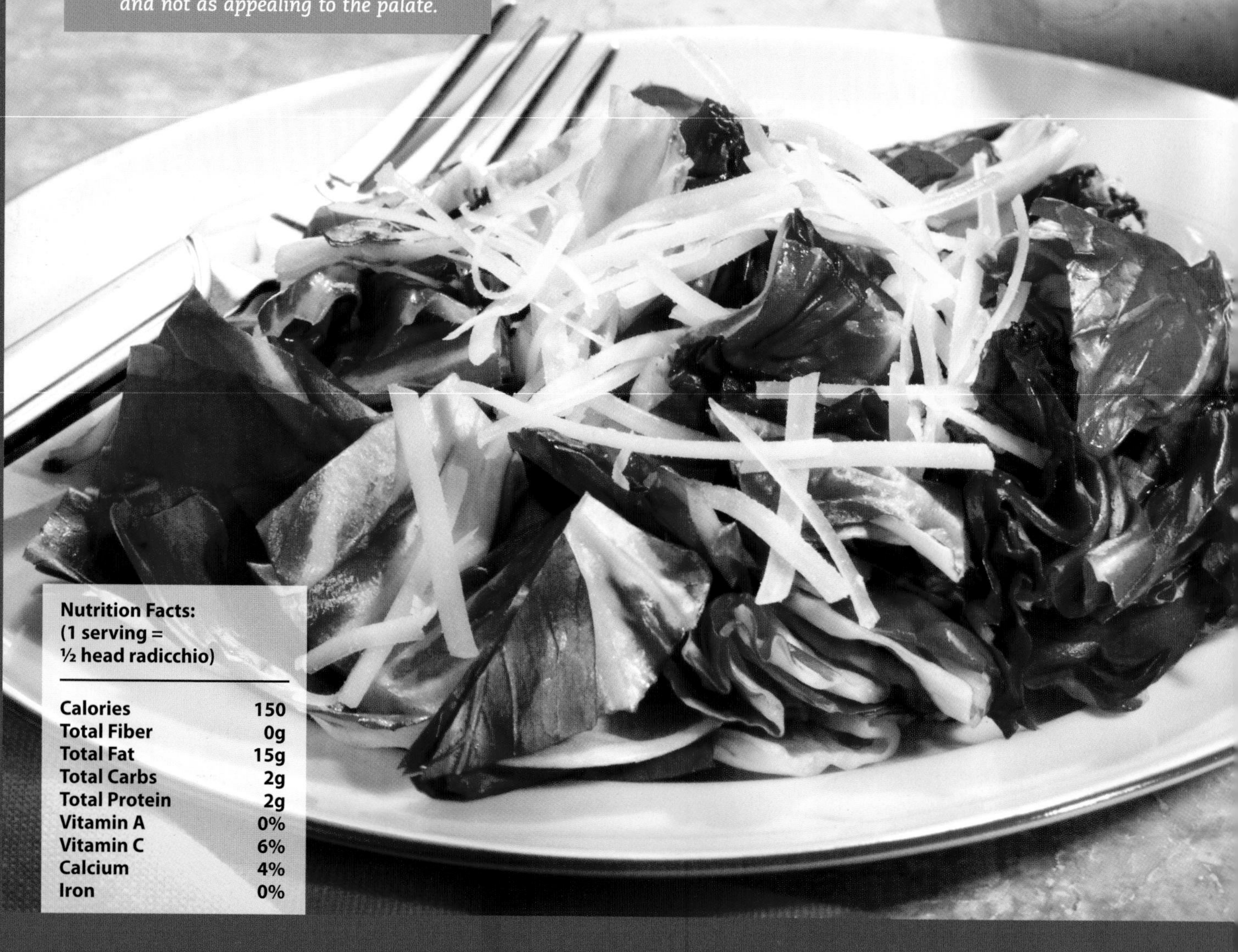

Nutrition Facts:
(1 serving = ½ head radicchio)

Calories	150
Total Fiber	0g
Total Fat	15g
Total Carbs	2g
Total Protein	2g
Vitamin A	0%
Vitamin C	6%
Calcium	4%
Iron	0%

GRILLED-CORN AND TOMATO SALAD

3 ears corn on the cob, shucked

1 cup quartered cherry tomatoes

½ red onion, julienned

½ cup ribbon-cut basil

¼ cup extra-virgin olive oil

1 lemon, juiced

Salt and pepper to taste

Preheat grill to medium. Grill the corn, turning often, until it is lightly colored and has grill marks, about 8–10 minutes. Remove the corn from the cob.

Gather all of the ingredients except the salt and pepper together in a bowl, and lightly toss to coat with the lemon and oil. Season with salt and pepper to taste, and serve.

3

SALADS

Nutrition Facts:
(1 serving = ¾ cup)

Calories	220
Total Fiber	3g
Total Fat	15g
Total Carbs	21g
Total Protein	3g
Vitamin A	15%
Vitamin C	30%
Calcium	2%
Iron	4%

4 Seafood

You may have heard the old joke "I am on a seafood diet... whenever I see food, I eat it!" I think we have already established that is not the best strategy when it comes to weight loss, but in fact, eating more fish is a great strategy when it comes to weight and well-being.

70 Ginger Grilled Lobster, Dr. Christopher S. Ahmad

72 Arctic Char with Pepper Guacamole

73 Sugar-Cane-Skewered, Tequila-Lime-Marinated Shrimp

74 Grilled Seafood Paella

75 Grilled Oysters with White-Wine-and-Bell-Pepper Mignonette Sauce

76 Chili-Rubbed Tuna with Pepper Yogurt Sauce

77 Cedar-Plank-Grilled Salmon Fillet with Mustard-Dill-and-Cannellini-Bean Sauce

78 Sea Bass with Tropical Salsa

79 Lemongrass Shrimp "Lollipops"

80 Mediterranean Whole Fish with Tomato-Artichoke Bruschetta

82 Chive-Pesto-Marinated Salmon Steaks

83 Artichoke-Miso-Sauce-Marinated Cod

84 Vegetable-and-Scallop Ceviche

85 Grilled Scallops with Green-Curry Lentils

86 Blackened Salmon with Grilled Maple Butternut Squash

87 Grilled Clams with Spinach and Celery

The omega-3 fatty acids found in fish are the healthiest of fats that can be consumed and have been linked to keeping our hearts and brains healthy. Fish highest in omega-3 are the fattier species such as salmon, trout, sardine, herring, mackerel, and oyster. The role of omega-3 fatty acids is still being studied, but omega-3 acids

- Have been shown to reduce symptoms of depression,
- May reduce the risk of ADHD, Alzheimer's, and dementia,
- May reduce inflammatory processes in the body.

Science continues to discover ways in which these essential fatty acids function during fetal brain, nerve, and vision development. Fish provides other nutrients, too, such as Vitamin D, B2 (riboflavin), calcium, zinc, magnesium, and potassium.

One traditional way to prepare and eat fish has been with butter sauces. Old school! The simplest way to prepare fish is to sprinkle on a little salt and pepper. The *Grill Yourself Skinny* recipes use lots of different spices—plus olive oil instead of butter to keep the fish as healthy and delicious as can be. The general guideline for grilling fresh fish is to allow 10 minutes for each inch of thickness; grill until the fish separates easily with a fork.

Butter as an accompaniment is what first may come to mind for the uninspired when thinking lobster. Unfortunately for the health and weight conscious, one 1.5-ounce serving of melted butter is 350 calories and 38 grams of fat. That is before you add any food! You will see in the featured recipe by New York Yankees Team Doctor and orthopedic surgeon Chris Ahmad a whole new twist with a Ginger Grilled Lobster. Ginger is a traditional spice that may also decrease inflammation and reduce muscle soreness. The lobster is succulent—and weighs in at far fewer calories and much less fat without all of that butter.

Consuming fish just two to three times a week is all that is needed to reap the health benefits described. Substituting higher-calorie proteins with fish will also go a long way in helping you lose weight and keep it off!

To find a great, regularly updated pocket guide to which fish are safest to eat regionally, check out:
http://www.montereybayaquarium.org/cr/cr_seafoodwatch/download.aspx

Considering that just 1.5-ounce serving of melted butter (like the kind you get at Red Lobster) is 350 calories, this tasty, creative, and simple grilled lobster is brilliant!

Nutrition Facts (1 serving = 1 lobster)			
Calories	436	Vitamin A	6%
Total Fiber	0g	Vitamin C	4%
Total Fat	18.5g	Calcium	60%
Total Carbs	2g	Iron	10%
Total Protein	54g		

GINGER GRILLED LOBSTER

4 whole lobsters (1–2 pounds each)

6 tablespoons finely chopped fresh ginger

3 tablespoons roughly cut ginger

6 cloves garlic, finely chopped

2 cloves garlic, whole

6 tablespoons canola oil

3 tablespoons rice wine vinegar

1 teaspoon crushed red pepper flakes

1 tablespoon softened butter

Salt and pepper to taste

4

SEAFOOD

In a small bowl whisk together the canola oil, rice vinegar, finely chopped ginger, finely chopped garlic, and crushed red pepper. Let the marinade stand while you cook.

Preheat grill to high. While the grill is heating up, drop the lobsters, one at a time, into large pot of boiling water. Cover, and cook 6 minutes. (Lobsters will not be fully cooked.) Transfer the lobsters to a cutting board. With the shell side down, place the tip of large knife in the center of the lobster, and cut it lengthwise in half to the head and then repeat from center through to end of the tail, but do not cut through the other side of the shell. Gently crack the large claws to allow access for marinade, but do not remove the shells. After allowing the lobsters to cool slightly, hinge them open; evacuate the body of the tomalley; and place the whole cloves of garlic and roughly cut ginger into the prepared cavity. Pour the marinade into the split tail, reserving a small amount to place into the large claws. Wrap each lobster in aluminum foil, sealing the edges by rolling foil over several times upon itself. Place the wrapped lobsters on the grill, and allow them to steam at high for 6–8 minutes. Remove the lobsters from the foil; lightly brush the tail meat with the softened butter; and season with salt and pepper. Place the cut side down on the grill to achieve a final char from the direct grill heat for 1–2 minutes. Remove the lobsters from grill; arrange them on a platter; and sprinkle them with chopped scallions.

Christopher S. Ahmad, MD, is Associate Professor, Orthopaedic Surgery, Columbia University, and Associate Attending Orthopaedic Surgery, New York Presbyterian Hospital. He specializes in shoulder instability and labral tears, rotator cuff pathology, ACL injuries, Tommy John surgery, and advanced arthroscopic surgical techniques for sports-related injuries of the knee, shoulder, and elbow. He is the Head Team Physician for The New York Yankees and a member of the MLB Team Physicians Association. He is also Head Team Physician for the 17 varsity teams fielded by the City College of New York as well as for several high schools in Manhattan and New Jersey. In addition, Dr. Ahmad serves as a consultant to local metropolitan gymnastics and swim teams.

Personal Wellness: I enjoy leading a healthy, active lifestyle, so whenever possible I go for a run. One of my most enjoyable hobbies is cooking and playing with recipes to make them leaner and healthier while maintaining intense flavors; that way, I get to enjoy them more often!

4 Servings • Prep: 10–15 min. • Grill: 6–10 min.

ARCTIC CHAR WITH PEPPER GUACAMOLE

4 Arctic char fillets, 4 ounces each
   (You may substitute salmon.)
1 tablespoon chili pepper
Salt and pepper to taste
Cooking spray as needed

GUACAMOLE:

1 ripe avocado
1 teaspoon diced shallots
2 tablespoons fresh lime juice
½ cup cilantro
½ cup small-diced tri-color bell peppers,
1 teaspoon ground cumin
1 teaspoon ground coriander
Salt and pepper to taste

Preheat grill to high. Coat the char with the chili pepper, salt, and pepper. Spray the grill lightly with the cooking spray, and sear the fillets on a 45-degree angle with the grill, skin side up. After 2 minutes, turn the fillets 90 degrees, creating a diamond pattern on the fish. Flip to the skin side, and cook to desired doneness.

For the guacamole, place all of the ingredients in a bowl, and mash them together using a fork or whisk. Adjust the seasonings.

Serve the char with a heaping tablespoon of the guacamole on top.

NUTRITION 4-1-1: AVOCADO FOR HEALTH

On Average 53.3 million pounds of guacamole are eaten every year on Super Bowl Sunday. Did you know that an avocado has twice as much potassium as a banana? The source of a great, healthy fat, avocado slices are great on sandwiches or as a spread instead of cheese or mayonnaise.

Nutrition Facts
(1 serving = 1 fillet,
1 tablespoon guacamole)

Calories	180
Total Fiber	1g
Total Fat	9g
Total Carbs	2g
Total Protein	23g
Vitamin A	15%
Vitamin C	10%
Calcium	2%
Iron	6%

NUTRITION 4-1-1: ARCTIC CHAR

Arctic char is both freshwater and saltwater fish; it is a member of the trout and salmon family. Arctic Char is similar to salmon, although it is longer and more colorful. *Fun Fact:* Wild Arctic Char can reach 25 years of age.

SUGAR-CANE-SKEWERED, TEQUILA-LIME-MARINATED SHRIMP

Add all of the marinade ingredients to a blender, and purée until smooth (3–5 minutes on high). Using a knife, diagonally slice off ½ inch of the sugar-cane tip, creating a point so that you can skewer the shrimp. Arrange 4 shrimp per sugar-cane skewer, and lay them on a shallow plate. Pour the marinade over the shrimp, and marinate for 15–20 minutes.

Preheat grill to medium high. Grill the shrimp to your desired doneness, and serve garnished with sliced green onions. ◠

16 large shrimp (about a pound)

4 sugar-cane skewers (or bamboo skewers)

¼ cup thinly sliced green onions (scallions)

MARINADE:

¼ cup olive oil

¼ cup tequila

¼ cup lime juice, freshly squeezed

2 shallots, roughly chopped

1 tablespoon dark-brown sugar

1 cup yellow cherry tomatoes

Salt and freshly ground black
   pepper to taste

4

SEAFOOD

Sugar-cane skewers are delicious! You can chew on the fabulous sweet fibers, use them for grilling, or even use them as a swizzle stick in iced or hot drinks. They will keep fresh for days if you refrigerate them once opened. Available year round, sugar cane contains naturally sweet juice and can even be enjoyed as a snack. **NOTE:** Do not swallow cane pulp. Not recommended for anyone with braces.

Nutrition Facts
(1 serving =
1 skewer with 4 shrimp)

Calories	210
Total Fiber	1g
Total Fat	14g
Total Carbs	9g
Total Protein	5g
Vitamin A	2%
Vitamin C	20%
Calcium	2%
Iron	4%

GRILLED SEAFOOD PAELLA

12 ounces clam juice

¼ cup white wine

¼ teaspoon saffron threads

¼ teaspoon salt

1½ tablespoons vegetable oil (has a higher smoking point than olive oil)

¼ cup thinly sliced red pepper

¼ cup diced Spanish onion

2 cloves garlic, chopped finely

2 teaspoons smoked paprika

1 cup short-grain rice (Arborio)

¼ cup diced tomatoes (canned)

½ tablespoon capers

¼ pound large shrimp, peeled and deveined

½ pound small mussels, scrubbed and debearded

½ pound clams, scrubbed

½ pound squid, sliced ½ inch thick after grilling

½ pound cod (or any thick white fish)

SPICE RUB FOR COD:

⅛ teaspoon smoked paprika

⅛ teaspoon garlic powder

Pinch cayenne

⅛ teaspoon chili powder

⅛ teaspoon onion powder

Pinch salt

Pour all clam juice into a large bowl; stir in saffron; and let it infuse for 20 minutes. Preheat grill to medium.

Apply the dry rub evenly on the cod or white fish. (Before placing on the grill, spray well with cooking oil to prevent fish from sticking.) Grill all seafood until clams and mussels open up, fish becomes white and flaky, and squid is tender. Take the fish and seafood off grill, and set it aside.

Heat a paella pan on grill. Add 1 tablespoon of oil to the pan, and sauté the onion and peppers in the pan until the onion is softened, about 5 minutes. Stir in tomatoes, and cook, stirring often, 10 to 12 minutes. Stir in the remaining oil, and add garlic. Stir in the rice; then level by patting on it with a wooden spoon. Toast the rice for 2 minutes.

Pour the clam-and-saffron liquid over the rice. Maintain a steady simmer for 12 minutes, reducing heat. Cover the grill, and cook until rice is al dente, 6 to 10 minutes.

Remove the paella from grill; let it stand about 5 minutes; then distribute the seafood over the paella before serving.

Nutrition Facts
(1 serving = ½ cup of cooked rice with seafood)

Calories	520
Total Fiber	2g
Total Fat	10g
Total Carbs	54g
Total Protein	49g
Vitamin A	25%
Vitamin C	60%
Calcium	15%
Iron	110%

No need to add much at all to this full meal as is but a simple green salad and a glass of sangria! Keep your rice portion to ½ cup.

GRILLED OYSTERS WITH WHITE-WINE-AND-BELL-PEPPER MIGNONETTE SAUCE

Preheat grill to high. Mix the ingredients for the mignonette sauce in a bowl. Once grill is heated, place the oysters on it, and immediately pour a teaspoon of the sauce on top of each oyster. Grill to desired doneness. (They will go quickly.)

Serve garnished with either parsley or green onions, a wedge of lemon, and a slice of bread. ⌐

8–12 oysters, freshly shucked
¼ cup chopped parsley or green onions (scallions)
1 lemon, wedged
4 pieces whole-wheat baguette, grilled

MIGNONETTE SAUCE

¼ cup dry white wine
1 tablespoon sherry or champagne vinegar
1 shallot, finely chopped
1 teaspoon extra-virgin olive oil
¼ cup finely chopped red bell peppers
Salt and pepper to taste

4 SEAFOOD

NUTRITION 4-1-1: OH, THOSE OYSTERS!

The oyster is an excellent source of zinc, an essential mineral that supports the immune system and healthy growth and development. The idea that they still might be aphrodisiacs is just a bonus. A group of shellfish that includes oysters was found to be rich in rare amino acids that trigger increased levels of sex hormones.

Although it's traditional to dip the bread and soak up the sauce, if you are trying to get skinny, skip that dipping! Add another oyster and a side salad for a more complete meal, or if you prefer, make a meal of appetizers and oysters.

Nutrition Facts (1 serving = 3–4 oysters, 1 tablespoon sauce) without baguette

Calories	130
Total Fiber	0g
Total Fat	4g
Total Carbs	8g
Total Protein	14g
Vitamin A	10%
Vitamin C	35%
Calcium	2%
Iron	45%

Nutrition Facts (1 serving = 3–4 oysters, 1 tablespoon sauce) with 1 slice of whole-wheat baguette per serving

Calories	220
Total Fiber	2g
Total Fat	4g
Total Carbs	27g
Total Protein	18g
Vitamin A	10%
Vitamin C	35%
Calcium	2%
Iron	50%

CHILI-RUBBED TUNA WITH PEPPER YOGURT SAUCE

4 ahi tuna steaks, 3–4 ounces each

Cooking spray as needed

SPICE BLEND

¼ cup chipotle chili powder

¼ cup ancho chili powder

2 tablespoons salt

1 tablespoon freshly ground black pepper

1 tablespoon finely chopped lime zest

PEPPER YOGURT SAUCE

½ cup peeled, seeded, and puréed grilled red bell pepper

½ cup low-fat or fat-free Greek yogurt

¼ cup low-fat or fat-free sour cream

2 tablespoons extra-virgin olive oil

2 tablespoons freshly squeezed lime juice

Salt and pepper to taste

Preheat grill to high. Mix the spice blend in a bowl. For the sauce, fold all ingredients together, and adjust seasoning. Generously coat each tuna steak with the spice blend, and lightly spray with cooking spray. Grill to desired doneness. (More rare is usually preferred.) Serve topped with a heaping tablespoon of the yogurt sauce.

Nutrition Facts (1 serving = 1 tuna steak with 1 tablespoon sauce)	
Calories	310
Total Fiber	0.5g
Total Fat	15g
Total Carbs	14g
Total Protein	32g
Vitamin A	160%
Vitamin C	45%
Calcium	10%
Iron	25%

Try pairing with the corn and tomato salad.

CEDAR-PLANK-GRILLED SALMON FILLETS WITH MUSTARD-DILL-AND-CANNELLINI-BEAN SAUCE

4 salmon fillets, 3-4 ounces each

4 pieces of picked dill

Salt and pepper to taste

Cedar planks, soaked in water or white wine as needed

MUSTARD-DILL-AND-CANNELLINI-BEAN SAUCE

1 cup cannellini beans (white kidney beans)

¼ cup Dijon mustard

¼ cup extra-virgin olive oil

¼ cup roasted garlic

1 lemon, juiced

Salt and pepper to taste

Water as needed

¼ cup finely chopped dill, with most of the stems removed

¼ cup low-fat or fat-free Greek Yogurt

4

SEAFOOD

NUTRITION 4-1-1: WHITE BEANS

Need a few reasons why you should incorporate white beans into your diet? How about the fact that they're low in fat, good source of protein and fiber, and excellent source of minerals and B vitamins.

This delicious dish would pair well with mushroom wraps.

Preheat one side of grill to high. For the sauce, place all of the ingredients (except for the dill and yogurt) in a blender, and purée on high until smooth. Adjust the consistency with water (if needed). Transfer to a grill-safe pan, and warm through using indirect heat. Place the cedar plank on the grill; season the salmon with salt and pepper; place a piece of dill on top of each piece of salmon; place the salmon on top of the cedar plank; and cover the grill. Cook the salmon to desired doneness, and remove from the heat.

To finish the sauce, remove from the heat, and stir in the yogurt and dill.

To serve, place a piece of salmon on a plate, and top with a tablespoon of the bean sauce. ∽

Nutrition Facts
(1 serving = 1 salmon fillet, 1 tablespoon sauce)

Calories	420
Total Fiber	6g
Total Fat	21g
Total Carbs	25g
Total Protein	30g
Vitamin A	2%
Vitamin C	10%
Calcium	8%
Iron	15%

SEA BASS WITH TROPICAL SALSA

4 sea bass fillets, 3–4 ounces each
Salt, pepper, and freshly ground cumin to taste
Cooking spray as needed

Mix all of the salsa ingredients in a bowl, and let it sit for 15 minutes to 2 hours under refrigeration.

Preheat grill to high. Season the fish, and lightly spray with cooking spray. Carefully grill the bass until it reaches desired doneness. Serve topped with a generous portion of the tropical salsa.

TROPICAL SALSA

½ cup finely diced tomatoes
¼ cup finely diced red bell pepper
¼ cup finely diced red onion
¼ cup finely diced cucumber, finely diced
2 tablespoons finely diced jalapeño pepper (optional)
2 tablespoons olive oil
½ cup medium-diced pineapple
¼ cup medium-diced mango
¼ cup chopped cilantro
2 tablespoons chopped mint
¼ cup lime juice
Salt and pepper to taste

Nutrition Facts (1 serving = 1 fillet, 2-3 tablespoons of salsa)	
Calories	130
Total Fiber	0g
Total Fat	3.5g
Total Carbs	2g
Total Protein	21g
Vitamin A	6%
Vitamin C	10%
Calcium	2%
Iron	2%

LEMONGRASS SHRIMP "LOLLIPOPS"

1 pound shrimp, small to medium in size

2 garlic cloves, roughly chopped

1 shallot, roughly chopped

1 tablespoon grated ginger

1 tablespoon olive oil

1 teaspoon salt

1 teaspoon finely grated black pepper

¼ cup shredded coconut, unsweetened, toasted
    until light brown

¼ cup chopped cilantro

2 jalapeño peppers, seeded, finely diced

1 lime, juiced

Rice flour or cornstarch as needed

8–10 lemongrass stalks, trimmed so that only
    the white part remains

Cooking spray as needed

Soy sauce, low sodium, as needed (optional)

Purée the shrimp, garlic, shallots, ginger, oil, salt, and pepper in a food processor until just slightly chunky. Transfer to a bowl, and fold in coconut, cilantro, peppers, and lime. Add rice flour or cornstarch, a little at a time, until the mixture starts to hold the form of a meatball. Mold a portion of the shrimp mix around each lemongrass stalk, leaving just enough of the lemongrass to hold like a stick.

Preheat one side of grill on high, leaving the other half off or on low. Place a piece of aluminum foil on the cool side of the grill; spray with oil; and arrange the lollipops so that all of them fit. Cover the grill, and cook for 5-10 minutes, or until the shrimp starts to "set."

Reapply spray, and transfer the lollipops from the aluminum foil to the hot side of the grill to sear. Cook to desired doneness, and serve lightly drizzled with the soy sauce. ⌐∾

Nutrition Facts (1 serving = 2 "lollipops")	
Calories	170
Total Fiber	1g
Total Fat	8g
Total Carbs	7g
Total Protein	16g
Vitamin A	6%
Vitamin C	25%
Calcium	6%
Iron	2%

MEDITERRANEAN WHOLE FISH WITH TOMATO-ARTICHOKE BRUSCHETTA

4 1½-to-2-pound rainbow trout or red
snapper, whole fish (gutted, scales
   removed, and rinsed)
Cooking spray as needed

MARINADE

2 lemons, juiced

2 tablespoons extra-virgin olive oil

2 sprigs fresh rosemary

2 tablespoons chopped fresh marjoram
   (or oregano)

Salt and black pepper to taste

BRUSCHETTA

7 Roma tomatoes, grilled

1 small can or bottle artichokes, grilled

½ cup sliced (into thin ribbons) fresh basil

2 cloves garlic, chopped very fine

¼ red onion, chopped fine

2½ tablespoons balsamic vinegar

1 tablespoon extra-virgin olive oil

Salt and black pepper to taste

Share the fish, one fillet per person, and enjoy with some appetizers or side vegetable and starches.

Combine all ingredients for marinade in two sealable plastic bags. Put two fish in each bag. Let the fish marinate in the refrigerator for 2 hours.

Preheat grill to medium. Grill tomatoes (whole) for 4–6 minutes and artichokes for 3–5 minutes. Remove from grill and let cool for 5 minutes. Remove skin and seeds from the tomatoes. Dice the artichokes and tomatoes, and place them in a medium-size bowl. Combine all of the other ingredients for the bruschetta in the bowl with the tomatoes and artichokes.

Turn grill up to medium high, and take the fish out of the refrigerator and the plastic bags. Before placing the fish on the grill, stuff it with the marinade from the bags. Spray the fish with cooking spray on both sides, and put the fish on the grill, about 6 minutes for each side.

When fish is fully cooked, remove it from grill. Serve it either family style or on individual plates, topped with bruschetta.

NUTRITION 4-1-1: POWERFUL OREGANO

At four times the antioxidant activity of blueberries and the highest among all herbs, oregano reigns supreme, but all herbs have something to offer in the way of powerful phytonutrient capacity.

Nutrition Facts
(1 serving = ½ whole fish)

Calories	280
Total Fiber	2g
Total Fat	12g
Total Carbs	8g
Total Protein	34g
Vitamin A	15%
Vitamin C	40%
Calcium	15%
Iron	8%

CHIVE-PESTO-MARINATED SALMON STEAKS

4 4-to-6-ounce salmon steaks or fillets

1 bunch fresh chives

¼ cup extra-virgin olive oil

¼ cup toasted pine nuts

2 garlic cloves, roasted

1 tablespoon Dijon mustard

⅛ teaspoon sea salt

Water as needed

Salt and pepper to taste

Lemon wedges as needed (optional)

Olive-oil cooking spray as needed

Blend together chives, oil, nuts, garlic, mustard, and sea salt in a blender. If the mixture doesn't blend, add small amounts of water until it does. Pour the mixture over the salmon, and let it sit for 10 minutes to 1 hour.

Preheat grill to medium high. Spray the fish with cooking spray, and grill it to desired doneness, 2 to 4 minutes per side. Serve immediately, topped with some fresh-squeezed lemon juice.

Delicious, but a bit rich between the healthy omega-3 fats in the salmon and the olive oil and pine nuts from the pesto. All are healthy fats, but this is, maybe, not so skinny. How do you convert a not-so-obviously skinny recipe into a skinny meal? Best served with a simple green salad and/or steamed vegetables.

Nutrition Facts
(1 serving =
1 salmon steak or fillet)

Calories	470
Total Fiber	6g
Total Fat	28g
Total Carbs	16g
Total Protein	36g
Vitamin A	2%
Vitamin C	2%
Calcium	4%
Iron	15%

ARTICHOKE-MISO-SAUCE-MARINATED COD

4 cod, sable, or halibut steaks (4–6 ounces each)

¼ cup miso (red, yellow, or white)

¼ cup drained-and-rough-chopped canned or jarred artichokes

2 shallots, peeled and minced

1 garlic clove, minced

2 tablespoons freshly grated ginger

½ to 1 teaspoon toasted sesame seed oil

1 tablespoon mirin (sweet rice cooking wine)

½ lime, juiced

1 tablespoon sake or dry white wine

Salt and pepper to taste

Cooking spray as needed

Add everything but the fish to a blender, and blend on high until perfectly smooth. The mixture should have enough salt, but taste and adjust as needed. Pour the mixture over the fish, and let it marinate for 1–3 hours.

Preheat grill to high. Grill the fish to desired doneness, and serve immediately. ✎

4

SEAFOOD

THIS IS SKINNY!
Pair with vegetable and side starch.

NUTRITION 4-1-1:
WILD-CAUGHT VS. FARM-RAISED FISH
Trying to decide if you should buy wild or farm-raised fish? Check out the Monterey Bay Aquarium Seafood Watch to help you make the right choice.

Nutrition Facts
(1 serving = 1 steak, 1–2 tablespoons of sauce)

Calories	140
Total Fiber	0g
Total Fat	1.5g
Total Carbs	2g
Total Protein	27g
Vitamin A	0%
Vitamin C	4%
Calcium	2%
Iron	2%

4 Servings • Prep: 15–20 min. • Refrigerate: 1 hr. to overnight • Grill: 5–10 min.

VEGETABLE-AND-SCALLOP CEVICHE

12–16 ounces bay scallops, cleaned

½ cup grilled and chopped red onion

½ cup grilled and chopped green bell pepper

½ cup grilled and chopped tomatoes (heirlooms if possible)

½ cup chopped cilantro

¼ cup finely diced jalapeño peppers

1 lemon, juiced

1 lime, juiced

1 orange, juiced

½ grapefruit, juiced

1 tablespoon freshly ground cumin

1 tablespoon freshly ground coriander

Salt and freshly ground black pepper to taste

Baked whole-grain tortilla chips as needed

Preheat grill to medium. Grill the onion, pepper, and tomatoes until they have grill marks and are just getting softened; then chop them. Fold all ingredients together in a bowl, and refrigerate for at least 1 hour to overnight. Serve with whole-grain-corn tortilla chips. ⌦

Note: this mixture must have enough "juice" to cover the scallops; the acid in the juice is what "cooks" them. If your citrus juice yield is not enough to cover the scallops, be sure to juice more until the scallops are covered. Do not make more than 48 hours before you plan to serve.

With or without the tortilla chips ...pair with a starch or vegetable.

Nutrition Facts
(1 serving =
3–4 scallops with 5 chips)

Calories	220
Total Fiber	5g
Total Fat	4.5g
Total Carbs	30g
Total Protein	16g
Vitamin A	15%
Vitamin C	130%
Calcium	8%
Iron	8%

Nutrition Facts
(1 serving = 3–4 scallops
without chips)

Calories	150
Total Fiber	4g
Total Fat	1g
Total Carbs	21g
Total Protein	15g
Vitamin A	15%
Vitamin C	130%
Calcium	6%
Iron	6%

GRILLED SCALLOPS WITH GREEN-CURRY LENTILS

20 large scallops

½ tablespoon salt

½ tablespoon black pepper

1 tablespoon canola oil

1 16-ounce can lentil beans

2 tablespoons ground peanuts (optional for garnish)

GREEN CURRY

1 cup cilantro leaves and stems

¼ cup basil leaves

½ lemongrass stalk, sliced thinly (using only the middle; cut off bottom and top)

5–6 cloves garlic

½ teaspoon turmeric

1½ teaspoons ground cumin

1 teaspoon ground cardamom

1 teaspoon ground coriander

1 tablespoon fresh ginger

1 can light coconut milk

1 cup vegetable stock

3 tablespoons light-brown sugar or cane sugar

½ tablespoon fish sauce

2 Kaffir lime leaves

1 teaspoon chili-garlic sauce

4

SEAFOOD

Preheat grill to medium high. Blend all green-curry ingredients together in a blender until it becomes a purée. Heat a saucepan on the grill. Pour the green-curry purée into the saucepan, and cook for 20 minutes. Take the saucepan off the grill, and strain the purée into a bowl. (This way, the curry is smooth.)

Empty and drain lentils out of the can into a strainer, and rinse well. Mix the lentils with the green curry, and set aside until ready to serve. (The green curry will be hot enough to warm up the lentils.)

Pat the scallops dry on a towel or paper towel. Season them with oil, salt, and pepper. Grill scallops on direct heat, grilling each side for 2–3 minutes. Take the scallops off the grill, and serve them over the green-curry lentils. Garnish with ground peanuts. ⌒

This is complete as is; if you would like, enjoy it with a nice glass of wine or dessert.

Nutrition Facts
(1 serving = 5 scallops, 4 ounces of lentils)

Calories	300
Total Fiber	9g
Total Fat	11g
Total Carbs	34g
Total Protein	18g
Vitamin A	8%
Vitamin C	4%
Calcium	4%
Iron	6%

BLACKENED SALMON WITH GRILLED MAPLE BUTTERNUT SQUASH

1½ pounds wild salmon fillet or Arctic char, skin on

1 large butternut squash, washed

1½ teaspoons salt

1½ tablespoons maple syrup

Cooking spray as needed

BLACKENED SEASONING

1 teaspoon ground white pepper

1 teaspoon garlic powder

1 teaspoon onion powder

1 teaspoon ground chili powder

1 teaspoon dried oregano

1 teaspoon paprika

1 teaspoon ground black pepper

1½ tablespoons canola oil (so salmon does not stick to grill)

Preheat grill to medium high. Peel the squash, and cut off the top and bottom. Slice in half lengthwise; scoop out pulp and seeds; and discard. (Keep the seeds, and roast them for a snack!) Slice the squash into long slices from top to bottom about 1 inch thick; season with salt; spray with cooking spray; place on the grill; and grill each side for 5–10 minutes or until fork tender. Take the squash off the grill; cut it into ½-inch cubes; and drizzle it with maple syrup.

Combine and mix all of the ingredients for the blackened rub in a small bowl. Brush the salmon with 1 tablespoon of oil, and rub the entire salmon fillet with the blackened seasoning. Before putting the salmon on the grill, brush the grill grates with the remaining oil. Place the salmon on the grill, skin side down.

Close the grill (so it acts like an oven for even cooking); grill for 4–5 minutes; then gently turn the salmon over and grill for another 4–5 minutes. Take the salmon off the grill, and set it aside to rest for 10 minutes. If the salmon seems slightly raw in the center, don't worry; it will continue to cook while resting.

Remove the skin from the salmon before serving it with lemon slices. ✎

Serve this tasty dish with a vegetable and salad.

Nutrition Facts (1 serving = 4 ounces of salmon, ¼ butternut squash)	
Calories	370
Total Fiber	3g
Total Fat	16g
Total Carbs	21g
Total Protein	35g
Vitamin A	250%
Vitamin C	40%
Calcium	10%
Iron	15%

GRILLED CLAMS WITH SPINACH AND CELERY

20–24 clams, shucked and chopped (shells reserved)

2 garlic cloves, finely chopped

2 tablespoons extra-virgin olive oil

½ cup baby spinach

½ cup finely diced red bell pepper

¼ cup peeled and finely diced celery

2 slices turkey bacon, crisped and finely diced

½ cup whole-wheat bread crumbs

Salt and pepper to taste

Cedar planks, soaked in water or wine (optional) as needed

1 lemon, wedged

Sauté the garlic in the oil until it starts to brown. Add the baby spinach, peppers, celery, and bacon, and cook until the spinach wilts and most of the excess liquid evaporates. Transfer the mixture to a bowl to cool for 10–15 minutes.

Add the bread crumbs to the bowl; adjust the seasoning; add the raw chopped clams; and mix one last time.

Preheat grill to high. Divide the stuffing among the reserved clamshells. Place wood planks on the grill and then place the stuffed clamshells on top of the planks. Cover the grill; cook until the clam filling is fully cooked or to your desired doneness; and serve with lemon wedges. ∽

4

SEAFOOD

You can always eat these clams as an appetizer instead of an entrée. If you keep the dish as an entrée, then make it a complete meal with a starch or vegetable.

Nutrition Facts:
(1 serving = 5–6 clams)

Calories	220
Total Fiber	2g
Total Fat	11g
Total Carbs	14g
Total Protein	17g
Vitamin A	20%
Vitamin C	50%
Calcium	6%
Iron	10%

5 Poultry

Does chicken come to mind first when someone says "poultry"? Chicken has become many people's alternative to red meat—leaner and protein packed. But of course, there is more to poultry than chicken.

90 Chipotle Turkey Tenderloin with Roasted-Corn-and-Black-Bean Salsa, Chef Angelo Basilone

92 Turkey Drumstick with Apple-Maple BBQ Sauce

93 Turkey-and-Coconut Meatballs with Spicy Peanut Sauce

94 Honey-Mustard BBQ Turkey

95 Wild-Rice-Stuffed Chicken Breast with Maple-Butternut-Squash Sauce

96 Tandoori Spice-Rubbed Chicken

97 Brick Chicken

98 Grilled Chicken Salad

99 Shredded Chicken with Grilled Corn Cakes

100 Chicken Fajita

102 Chicken Souvlaki with Cucumber Sauce on Whole-Wheat Pita

103 Chicken Meatball Kebabs with Mango-Papaya Sauce

104 Tea-Spice Duck breast

105 Duck with Cherry-Port-Wine sauce

106 Duck with Plum Sauce

108 Ostrich Open-Faced Sandwich with Sundried Tomatoes and Chimichurri Sauce

109 Ostrich with Jicama Slaw

All That Is Poultry (or Not)

In this chapter, chicken, turkey, duck, and ostrich are all featured. Skinless chicken and turkey are lean proteins. So is duck, again as long as you don't eat the skin (unfortunately, most people's favorite part).

But Ostrich? Aghast at Ostrich? Give it a try. Ostrich is a bird, but it is actually not considered poultry. Rather, it is part of a species that includes the Rhea, Cassowary, and Emu. Its flesh is more like a red meat, yet it's even leaner than chicken. Ostrich is rich in iron—the oxygen-carrying component of blood and an important nutrient that helps your immune system work. Women, in particular, tend to need more iron from their diet.

Aim for Variety

Most people tend to fall back on chicken, and eating the same food all of the time can get old. If you are eating chicken at almost every meal, change it up! Try to rethink menu planning. If you eat three meals plus snacks each day, that gives you 21 meals to create. Try planning so that you eat your protein from some variation of

- chicken four times a week
- turkey a few times a week
- fish three times a week
- red meat once or twice a week
- ostrich and duck once in a while
- eggs a few times a week
- soy- or bean-based dishes a few times a week
- dairy most days

Also, keep vegetables abundant. Your meal plan will be complete, varied, and satisfying. You'll feel better and healthier—and you'll be weight-smart!

**8 Servings • Prep: 20–25 min. • Marinate: 15 min.–2 hrs.
• Grill: 16–20 min. (until internal temp. is at least 165°F) • Rest: 10 min.**

NUTRITION 4-1-1: ANTIOXIDANT BLACK BEANS
Black beans' dark pigments contain the highest level of flavonoids and greatest antioxidant activity of all common varieties.

I worked with Chef Angelo when he joined the Giants football organization. All of the players and the entire staff love his food, presentation, and style.

Nutrition Facts:	Calories	299	Vitamin A	40%
(1 serving =	Total Fiber	4.5g	Vitamin C	65%
3 ounces of	Total Fat	14g	Calcium	2%
turkey)	Total Carbs	22g	Iron	12.5%
	Total Protein	25g		

CHIPOTLE TURKEY TENDERLOIN WITH ROASTED-CORN-AND-BLACK-BEAN SALSA

1½ pounds turkey tenderloin
2 chipotle peppers in adobo
1 clove garlic
1 shallot
½ bunch cilantro
2 tablespoons honey
1 teaspoon Dijon mustard
2 tablespoons canola oil
1 lime, juiced
Salt and pepper to taste
Cooking spray as needed

SALSA
¼ pound cooked black beans
3 ears corn, cut fresh from the cob
½ red onion, diced small
1 red bell pepper, diced small
1 poblano pepper, roasted and diced small
2 Roma tomatoes, diced small
1 teaspoon ground cumin
1 tablespoon chipotle chili powder
2 tablespoons olive oil
4 ounces tomato Juice
2 limes, juiced
½ bunch cilantro, chopped
Salt and pepper to taste

Combine all of the main ingredients except the turkey and cooking spray in a food processor, and grind into a paste. Generously rub the turkey tenderloins with the mixture, and let them sit for 15 minutes at room temperature or refrigerate for at least 2 hours.

For the salsa, mix the corn, red onion, and red pepper in a small bowl with the cumin, chili powder, and olive oil, and lay the mixture flat on a sheet pan. Roast it in a 450°F oven for 12 minutes. Remove the mixture from the oven; fold in the remaining ingredients; and adjust the seasoning. You will serve the roasted salsa with the turkey tenderloins at room temperature.

Preheat grill to medium high. Spray the tenderloins lightly with cooking spray, and grill them for about 8 minutes per side. Cook to an internal temperature of at least 165°F. Let the tenderloins sit for 10 minutes before slicing. ✳

As a lifelong New York Giants fan, Chef Angelo Basilone is thrilled to lead the culinary team at the Timex Performance Training Center Cafe for the New York Football Giants, cooking for the team he has rooted for his entire life. He graduated from the world-renowned Culinary Institute of America, in Hyde Park, NY, in 1997. After graduating, Chef Angelo joined Flik International to further build on his management and culinary skills, working with such high-profile businesses such as Honeywell, MBNA Bank, and The Archdiocese Center of Newark. He has also lent his culinary expertise to the classic La Pastaria Ristorante in Summit, NJ, and the esteemed Highlawn Pavilion in West Orange, NJ.

Personal wellness: I try to make smart choices and find time to exercise to stay fit. Limiting portion sizes and using the right cooking techniques are key to maintaining a healthy lifestyle. You cannot go wrong with a grilled lean protein!

**4 Servings • Prep: 20–25 min. • Simmer: 5–10 min.
• Grill: 15–20 min. (until internal temp. is at least 165°F) • Rest: 5 min.**

TURKEY DRUMSTICK WITH APPLE-MAPLE BBQ SAUCE

4 small turkey drumsticks

1 tablespoon vegetable oil

½ cup rough-chopped red onion

1 clove garlic, minced

½ cup applesauce

½ cup ketchup

¼ cup maple syrup

¼ cup molasses

¼ cup low-sodium chicken stock

1 lemon, juiced

1 tablespoon Worcestershire sauce

1 teaspoon freshly ground black pepper

1 teaspoon ground chili powder

1 pinch ground cumin

Salt and pepper to taste

Cooking spray as needed

Note: Each serving should use ¼ cup of sauce. This recipe will make more than 1 cup of sauce. You can refrigerate extra sauce for a week or keep it frozen for longer.

Pour the oil in a saucepan, and sauté the onions and garlic until the onions become translucent. Add the applesauce, ketchup, syrup, molasses, and chicken stock, and let it simmer for 5–10 minutes. Finish the sauce with the lemon juice, Worcestershire sauce, ground black pepper, chili, and cumin, and then add salt to taste. (This sauce can be made up to 5 days in advance if you keep it under refrigeration.)

Preheat grill to high. Season the drumsticks with salt and pepper; brush them with BBQ sauce you made; and grill on high until marked on both sides. Reduce the heat to low, and continue to cook until the turkey reaches an internal temperature of at least 165°F (175°F if you don't like medium-rare to rare). Let the turkey rest, off the heat, for at least 5 minutes, and serve on the bone. ✳

The serving size of a drumstick makes this choice 440 calories with three times the amount of protein than many of the other entrées feature. If you just love biting into a drumstick or find yourself with some other entrée that is over 400 calories before appetizers or side dishes, keep it simple. Watch which appetizers or sides you choose. You can eat your drumstick and still come in calorically OK as long as you carefully select everything else; otherwise, your meal can easily climb to 800 calories or more.

Nutrition Facts: (1 serving = 1 turkey drumstick, ¼ cup of sauce)

Calories	440
Total Fiber	0g
Total Fat	9g
Total Carbs	18g
Total Protein	67g
Vitamin A	4%
Vitamin C	10%
Calcium	6%
Iron	35%

4 Servings • Prep: 20–25 min. • Simmer: 10–15 min.
• Grill: 10–15 min. (until internal temp. is at least 165°F)

93

TURKEY-AND-COCONUT MEATBALLS WITH SPICY PEANUT SAUCE

¾–1 pound lean ground turkey

1 large egg

¼ cup finely chopped red onion

¼ cup low-sodium soy sauce

1 clove garlic, very finely chopped

¼ cup chopped fresh cilantro

¼ cup finely chopped fresh mint leaves

Bread crumbs as needed, Japanese style (panko) preferred

1 tablespoon sambal oelek sauce (optional for spicy heat)

1 teaspoon fish sauce (optional for savory umami taste)

Cooking Spray as needed

4 bamboo skewers, soaked in water

Lettuce as needed (shredded optional)

SAUCE

½ cup peanut butter, chunky or smooth

¼ cup rice wine vinegar

½ cup low-fat coconut milk

¼ cup soy sauce

1 tablespoon crushed dried red chilies

1 tablespoon lime juice, freshly squeezed

1 tablespoon grated ginger

½ teaspoon ground cumin

In a bowl, mix all of the ingredients for the meatballs, adding enough bread crumbs to bind the meatballs together. Form 12–16 meatballs, and skewer them 3–4 meatballs per skewer. Preheat grill to medium high. Spray the skewers with cooking spray, and carefully grill them until they reach an internal temperature of at least 165°F.

In a saucepan on medium heat, melt the peanut butter with the vinegar, coconut milk, and soy. Add the chilies, lime, ginger, and cumin, and lightly simmer over low heat for 10–15 minutes. Taste, and adjust seasonings if necessary.

Serve the meatballs over lettuce (shredded if you like), drizzled with about 1 tablespoon of the peanut sauce. ✳

You might use this as an appetizer, or pair it with sweet potato and grill-top stir-fry (or simply a grilled vegetable).

5

POULTRY

Nutrition Facts: (1 serving = 1 skewer of 3–4 meatballs, 1 tablespoon sauce)

Calories	190
Total Fiber	1g
Total Fat	8g
Total Carbs	4g
Total Protein	25g
Vitamin A	6%
Vitamin C	2%
Calcium	2%
Iron	15%

6 Servings • Prep: 5–10 min.
• Grill: 15–20 min. (until internal temp. is at least 165°F) • Rest: 5 min. or more

HONEY-MUSTARD BBQ TURKEY

1½ pounds turkey breast, trussed

½ cup honey, wild if possible

¼ cup Dijon or yellow mustard

¼ cup apple-cider vinegar

Salt and pepper to taste

Cooking spray as needed

Mix the honey, mustard, vinegar, and seasonings in a bowl, and whisk until smooth and well incorporated. Season the turkey; then generously brush it with the honey-mustard BBQ sauce.

Preheat grill to high, and sear the turkey until it's marked. Immediately reduce the heat to low, and continue to cook until the turkey reaches an internal temperature of at least 165°F. Let the turkey rest, off the heat, for at least 5 minutes; then slice and serve. ❉

This is low in neither calories nor carbohydrates, considering it is the protein portion only, so I must admit it is not a very skinny recipe. I usually prefer to go simple when it comes to flavoring my protein and eat my carbohydrates calories from whole grains or the occasional dessert, but this one tastes so good it is here as an option for those who just love the flavor. Green salad and simple vegetable are the way to round out here.

Nutrition Facts:
(1 serving = 4 ounces of turkey breast)

Calories	280
Total Fiber	0g
Total Fat	8g
Total Carbs	26g
Total Protein	25g
Vitamin A	0%
Vitamin C	0%
Calcium	2%
Iron	8%

4 Servings • Prep: 25–30 min.
• Grill: 15–20 min. (until internal temp. is at least 165°F) • Rest: 5 min. or more

95

WILD-RICE-STUFFED CHICKEN BREAST WITH MAPLE-BUTTERNUT-SQUASH SAUCE

4 3–4-ounce boneless chicken breasts

½ cup cooked quinoa

½ cup cooked wild rice

½ cup grilled cherry tomatoes

½ cup chopped parsley

¼ cup finely diced red onions

¼ cup toasted pine nuts

¼ cup dried cranberries

½ lemon, juiced

2 tablespoons blue cheese

Salt and pepper to taste

Cooking spray as needed

SAUCE

1 teaspoon extra-virgin olive oil

2 cups butternut squash; diced, peeled

½ cup chopped yellow onion

¼ cup chopped celery

⅛ teaspoon ground cardamom, nutmeg, or mace

1–2 cups vegetable or chicken stock (for thinning)

Maple syrup to taste

Sea salt and black pepper to taste

Using a paring knife, create a hollow cavity lengthwise inside the chicken breast, being careful not to pierce the sides. Mix all of the main ingredients (except the chicken and cooking spray) together, and place it inside a pastry piping bag or a heavy-duty sealable plastic bag. Inject the filling into the chicken breast by squeezing the mixture into the cavity.

For the sauce, toss the squash, onion, celery, and oil into a roasting pan. Bake at 325°F for 1½ hours. Place the roasted ingredients in a blender with the other sauce ingredients, and purée until smooth. Add more stock if necessary. Season to taste.

Preheat grill to high. Season the outside of the chicken; spray it lightly with cooking spray; and grill it on one side. When you flip the chicken, lower the heat or use indirect heat to finish cooking the breasts. Grill until the chicken reaches an internal temperature of at least 165°F. Remove the meat from the heat; let it rest for at least 5 minutes; then slice and serve with sauce. ❋

Add a side salad or some vegetables, and your meal is complete.

Note: Freeze leftover sauce in ice-cube trays, and store in sealable plastic bags until needed again.

NUTRITION 4-1-1: WONDERFUL WILD RICE

It may look like rice, but this nutty grain is actually the seed of marsh grass. One study found wild rice to have 30 times the anti-oxidant activity of white rice—reason enough to make the switch.

Nutrition Facts:
(1 serving =
1 stuffed chicken breast,
1 tablespoon sauce)

Calories	300
Total Fiber	6g
Total Fat	8g
Total Carbs	28g
Total Protein	27g
Vitamin A	40%
Vitamin C	50%
Calcium	20%
Iron	10%

4 Servings • Prep: 10 min. • Rest/Suffuse: 15–30 min.
• Grill: 10–15 min. (until internal temp. is at least 165°F) • Rest: 5 min or more

TANDOORI SPICE-RUBBED CHICKEN

4 skinless, boneless chicken breasts

4 tablespoons paprika, smoked variety preferred

2 tablespoons kosher salt

2 tablespoons freshly ground coriander

2 tablespoons freshly ground cumin

1 tablespoon light brown sugar

1 teaspoon freshly ground black pepper

1 teaspoon turmeric

1 teaspoon ground ginger

½ teaspoon ground cinnamon

½ teaspoon cayenne pepper (optional)

Cooking spray as needed

Mix all of the spices together in a bowl. Coat the chicken, and let it sit for 15–30 minutes.

Preheat grill to medium high. Lightly spray the chicken with cooking spray, and grill it until it reaches an internal temperature of at least 165°F. Remove the chicken from the heat; let it rest for at least 5 minutes; then slice and serve. ❈

Nutrition Facts:
(1 serving =
1 chicken breast)

Calories	190
Total Fiber	4g
Total Fat	4.5g
Total Carbs	9g
Total Protein	27g
Vitamin A	50%
Vitamin C	4%
Calcium	6%
Iron	15%

BRICK CHICKEN

1 3–4-pound broiler-fryer chicken, quartered
2 tablespoons olive or canola oil
¼ cup chopped thyme leaves
Salt and pepper to taste
1 lemon, quartered
Cooking spray as needed

Preheat grill to high. Place two large cast-iron pans on the grill to preheat. Rub the chicken with the oil, thyme, salt, and pepper. Place the chicken, skin side down, in the pan, and place the other pan on top to press the chicken down. (You can instead use the more-traditional method: a brick wrapped in aluminum foil, below; hence, the name of the recipe.) When the first side develops a crust, flip the chicken in the pan, and continue to cook until it reaches an internal temperature of at least 165°F. Remove the chicken from the heat, and serve with a squeeze of lemon juice on each piece of chicken. ❄

5
POULTRY

Nutrition Facts:
(1 serving = ¼ chicken)

Calories	210
Total Fiber	1g
Total Fat	20g
Total Carbs	2g
Total Protein	5g
Vitamin A	4%
Vitamin C	15%
Calcium	2%
Iron	4%

GRILLED CHICKEN SALAD

¾ –1 pound grilled chicken breast, boneless & skinless, chopped

½ cup medium-diced Granny Smith apple

½ cup finely diced red onion

¼ cup finely diced carrot

¼ cup finely diced celery

½ lemon, juiced

½ cup low-fat or fat-free Greek yogurt

¼ cup low-fat mayonnaise

1 tablespoon Dijon mustard (optional)

¼ cup toasted and chopped pecans or almonds

Salt and Pepper to taste

Cooking spray as needed

8 tomato wheels

8 leaves romaine lettuce

Preheat grill to medium high. Lightly mist the chicken breasts with cooking spray so that they won't stick, and grill them to an internal temperature of at least 165°F. Remove them from the heat, and chop them into ½–¾-inch cubes. Mix the chicken and the rest of the salad ingredients together in a bowl. Evenly portion the salad onto eight leaves of romain lettuce; top with tomato (not shown); and serve. ❋

Nutrition Facts: (1 serving = 3–4 ounces of chicken breast, 2 lettuce leaves)

Calories	290
Total Fiber	5g
Total Fat	14g
Total Carbs	17g
Total Protein	29g
Vitamin A	70%
Vitamin C	20%
Calcium	8%
Iron	15%

4 Servings • Prep: 15–20 min.
• Grill: 30–35 min. (until internal temp. of chicken is at least 165°F) • Rest: 5 min.

99

SHREDDED CHICKEN WITH GRILLED CORN CAKES

Preheat grill to high heat. Cook the corn until it develops grill marks, not burned. (About 5 minutes on each side.) Take the corn off of the grill, and set aside to let cool. While the corn is cooling, rub spices onto the chicken thighs, making sure to evenly cover each piece. Put it in the refrigerator until it's ready to grill.

Cut the corn off of the cob, and put in a large bowl; then mix in all of the other ingredients for the corn cakes. Form pancakes, and sear the cakes in a hot skillet on the grill (using cooking spray to keep the cakes from sticking) until each side is nice and crispy (not burned), with the inside fluffy and soft. Place them on a baking sheet in an oven at 200°F to keep warm.

Take the chicken out of the refrigerator, and grill it until the internal temperature of each piece is at least 165°F. Take the chicken off the grill, and let it cool for 5 minutes. Using two forks, shred the chicken; then mix ingredients for the chipotle sour cream together in a bowl. Divide the shredded chicken into four portions; place each portion on top of a corn cake; top with a small dollop of chipotle sour cream; and garnish with chopped chives if desired. ❋

4 chicken thighs, fat trimmed

⅛ teaspoon cumin

Pinch cayenne pepper

½ teaspoon smoked sweet paprika

⅛ teaspoon onion powder

½ teaspoon garlic powder

¼ teaspoon ancho chili powder

¼ teaspoon salt

¼ teaspoon black pepper

CHIPOTLE SOUR CREAM

½ cup fat-free sour cream

1 tablespoon chipotle sauce

1 tablespoon chopped cilantro

CORN CAKES

1½ ears corn, husk removed

3 chives, chopped (plus some additional for garnish if desired)

½ cup all-purpose flour

½ teaspoon salt

¼ teaspoon baking soda

½ teaspoon Old Bay seasoning

1 egg white

¼ cup buttermilk

¼ cup 2% milk

It seems the thing that makes this recipe so unique and special is the corn cakes, but of course, you could put the shredded chicken on top of a salad.

Nutrition Facts:
(1 serving = 1 chicken thigh, 1 corn cake, 2½ tablespoons sour cream)

Calories	260
Total Fiber	2g
Total Fat	7g
Total Carbs	29g
Total Protein	21g
Vitamin A	10%
Vitamin C	6%
Calcium	10%
Iron	10%

Nutrition Facts:
(1 serving =
1 chicken breast)

Calories	360
Total Fiber	2g
Total Fat	19g
Total Carbs	8g
Total Protein	37g
Vitamin A	25%
Vitamin C	130%
Calcium	4%
Iron	6%

4 Servings • Prep: 20–25 min. • Marinate: 15–60 min.
• Grill: 15–20 min. (until internal temp. is at least 165°F) • Rest: 15 min.

101

CHICKEN FAJITA

4 4–6-ounce chicken breasts, skin removed
½ cup rough-chopped cilantro
¼ cup lime juice, fresh squeezed
3 cloves garlic, crushed and rough chopped
1 jalapeño pepper, seeded and rough chopped
4 tablespoons olive or canola oil
1 teaspoon ground coriander
1 teaspoon ground cumin
1 red bell pepper, cut into ¼-inch strips
1 green bell pepper, cut into ¼-inch strips
1 red or white onion, cut into ¼-inch strips
Salt and pepper to taste
Cooking spray as needed

OPTIONAL AS-NEEDED INGREDIENTS

Whole-grain tortillas
Low-fat or fat-free sour cream
Fresh salsa / pico de gallo salsa
Shredded lettuce
Brown rice
Guacamole

The optional add-ons can add flavor and/or a lot of calories depending on what you select. Go for tortilla or rice, not both; or try a tortilla-less fajita, and pile on the salsa with a hint of guacamole.

5

POULTRY

Mix the cilantro, lime, garlic, jalapeño, 2 tablespoons of oil, coriander, cumin, salt, and pepper in a bowl. Add the chicken, and let it marinate for 15 minutes to 1 hour.

Preheat grill to medium high. Toss the red and green peppers, onions, 2 tablespoons of oil, salt, and pepper in a bowl. Grill the chicken breasts to at least 165°F, and grill the onions and peppers in a perforated grilling pan to desired doneness. Set the chicken aside once done to rest for 15 minutes or so.

To assemble the fajitas, slice the chicken, and mix it with the grilled onions and peppers. Place the mixture on your favorite tortilla, and top with your preferred ingredients. (See above.) ✳

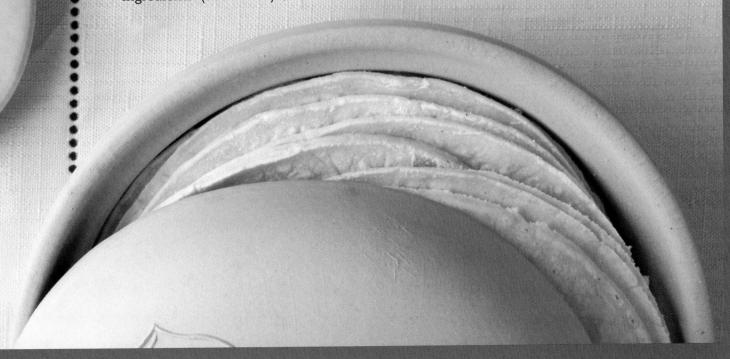

4 Servings • Prep: 10–15 min. • Marinate: 1 hr.
• Grill: 15–20 min. (until internal temp. is at least 165°F)

CHICKEN SOUVLAKI WITH CUCUMBER SAUCE ON WHOLE-WHEAT PITA

¾ pound boneless, skinless chicken breast,
    cut into 1-inch cubes

½ cup brown-rice vinegar

¼ cup olive oil

¼ cup lemon juice

1 tablespoon chopped fresh oregano

1 teaspoon chopped fresh mint

Salt and pepper to taste

4 pieces whole-wheat pita bread

Tomato, cut into wheels, as needed

White onion as needed

SAUCE

1 cup low-fat Greek yogurt

½ cup peeled, seeded, and diced cucumber

2 tablespoons brown-rice vinegar

1 tablespoon lemon Juice

1 tablespoon olive oil

¼ cup chopped fresh dill

1 teaspoon chopped garlic

Salt and pepper to taste

Combine ½ cup brown-rice vinegar, ¼ cup of oil, ¼ cup of lemon juice, oregano, mint, salt, and pepper in a bowl. Add the chicken, and let it marinate for 1 hour.

Preheat grill to high. Spray the chicken lightly with cooking spray, and sear the breasts until grill marks appear. Then turn down the heat to low, and cook until the breasts reach an internal temperature of at least 165°F.

Fold all of the sauce ingredients together in a bowl, and adjust the seasonings. Toast the pita bread on the grill; place desired amount of fresh onion and tomato on top, and cover with the grilled chicken and cucumber sauce. ✳

Nutrition Facts:
(1 serving = 3 ounces of chicken breast, 1 pita, 1 tablespoon sauce)

Calories	250
Total Fiber	2g
Total Fat	8g
Total Carbs	20g
Total Protein	26g
Vitamin A	2%
Vitamin C	6%
Calcium	6%
Iron	8%

6 Servings • Prep: 15–20 min. • Caramelize: 5–10 min.
• Grill: 30–35 min. (make sure internal temp. of meatballs is at least 165°F)

103

CHICKEN MEATBALL KEBABS WITH MANGO-PAPAYA SAUCE

1½ pounds ground chicken

10 cloves garlic, skin on

½ large yellow onion

1 teaspoon ground cumin

½ teaspoon ground coriander

2 tablespoons chopped fresh cilantro

½ cup whole-wheat panko bread crumbs

Salt and pepper to taste

4 metal skewers

Cooking spray as needed

SAUCE

1 cup frozen mango chunks

1 cup frozen papaya chunks

½ teaspoon chili garlic sauce

1 tablespoon rice wine vinegar

Preheat grill to medium high. Place the garlic cloves in aluminum foil; seal the foil, making a closed pouch; and poke a small hole in middle of the pouch. Place the garlic foil pouch on the grill for 20–25 minutes.

In the meantime, caramelize the onions in a small pan with some cooking spray. This can be done on the grill or a stove. Cook the onions until they are brown, soft, and sweet. When both the garlic and the onions are done, chop them up, and combine them in a large bowl. Mix in all other ingredients for the meatballs in the same bowl.

After all of the ingredients are well mixed, make the meatballs. Spray each meatball generously with cooking spray; assemble three or four (depending on the size) meatballs onto each skewer; and put the skewers on the grill. Cook about 5 minutes each side, until the middle is at least 165°F.

While the meatballs are on the grill, combine all of the ingredients for the sauce in a saucepan. Cook the sauce until the frozen mango and papaya become soft and the sauce comes to a boil. Take the sauce off the heat, and purée it using a blender. Serve the meatballs with the mango-papaya sauce drizzled on top (about 1½–2 tablespoons per skewer). ❈

NUTRITION 4-1-1: ENZYMATIC PAPAYA

Try a Thai green papaya salad for a refreshing side dish that aids in digestion. Papayas, especially the green variety, are high in the digestive enzymes papain and chymopapain.

Nutrition Facts:
(1 serving = 1 skewer of 3–4 meatballs, 1½–2 tablespoons sauce)

Calories	230
Total Fiber	2g
Total Fat	10g
Total Carbs	16g
Total Protein	22g
Vitamin A	10%
Vitamin C	40%
Calcium	2%
Iron	8%

TEA-SPICE DUCK BREAST

4 4–6-ounce duck breasts, skin removed

Contents of 2 tea bags (approx. 2 tablespoons), cherry, lemon, or raspberry flavored

1 teaspoon orange zest

½ teaspoon salt

½ teaspoon freshly ground pepper

½ teaspoon ground ginger powder

½ teaspoon onion powder

Cooking spray as needed

Preheat grill to high. Place the tea and all of the spices in a spice grinder or coffee grinder, and grind until it becomes a fine powder. Lightly dust the duck breasts with the tea spice. Grill the breasts on high until a crust forms; then immediately turn the heat as low as possible, and continue to cook to the desired doneness.

Let the duck breast rest, off the heat, for 5 minutes; slice; and serve. ✻

Nutrition Facts:
(1 serving =
1 duck breast)

Calories	210
Total Fiber	0g
Total Fat	7g
Total Carbs	1g
Total Protein	34g
Vitamin A	2%
Vitamin C	20%
Calcium	0%
Iron	45%

Note: You remove the skin because duck breast, per 100g serving, drops from 11g of fat to less than 3g of fat when the skin is removed (data from USDA nutrient database).

4 Servings • Prep: 20–25 min. • Grill: 10–15 min. • Rest: 5 min.

105

DUCK WITH CHERRY-PORT-WINE SAUCE

4 4–6-ounce duck breasts, skin removed

Salt and pepper to taste

4 green onions, thinly sliced on the bias

Cooking spray as needed

SAUCE

1 teaspoon olive or canola oil

1 cup halved pitted cherries

½ cup tawny (preferred) or ruby port

1 cup low-sodium chicken stock

½ tablespoon low-sodium soy sauce

1 fresh ginger root slice (to be removed at the end)

1 thyme sprig (to be removed at the end)

Preheat grill to high. Add the oil and cherries to a saucepan, and cook to soften. Remove the pan carefully from the heat, and add the port. At this point, any flames can cause the port to ignite. Be cautious of this.

When the port reduces by one-fourth, add the chicken stock, soy sauce, ginger, and thyme, and simmer to reduce by another one-fourth. Remove the ginger and thyme, and set aside for plating.

Season the duck, and lightly mist it with the cooking spray. Grill on high until just marked; then immediately reduce the heat to as low as possible, and cook to desired doneness. Let the duck breast rest, off the heat, for 5 minutes; slice; and serve topped with the port wine sauce. Garnish with the green onions, ginger, and thyme. ❄

Note: You remove the skin because duck breast, per 100g serving, drops from 11g of fat to less than 3g of fat when the skin is removed (data from USDA nutrient database).

Nutrition Facts:
(1 serving =
1 duck breast,
1 tablespoon sauce)

Calories	360
Total Fiber	7g
Total Fat	10g
Total Carbs	23g
Total Protein	37g
Vitamin A	8%
Vitamin C	25%
Calcium	4%
Iron	45%

DUCK WITH PLUM SAUCE

4 4–6-ounce duck breasts, skin removed

1 teaspoon kosher salt

½ teaspoon Chinese five-spice powder

¼ teaspoon freshly ground black pepper

4 ripe plums

1 teaspoon olive or canola oil

¼ cup finely diced red onion

2 cloves garlic, minced

1 jalapeño pepper, seeded & finely diced (optional)

¼ cup white wine

¼ cup applesauce

¼ cup orange juice

¼ cup low-sodium soy sauce

Cooking spray as needed

Preheat grill to high. Add the oil, onions, garlic, and peppers to a preheated saucepan, and sauté until the onions become translucent. Add the white wine, and reduce until almost dry. Reduce the heat. Dip the plums in boiling water for 30 seconds to a minute; then immediately remove to a bowl of ice water. This should allow you to easily peal off the skin. Dice the plums, and add them to the pan with the applesauce, juice, and soy sauce. Simmer the sauce to desired consistency, and set aside.

Combine the salt and spices in a bowl, and lightly coat the duck breasts. Grill the duck on high until just marked; then immediately reduce the heat as low as possible, and cook to desired doneness. Let the duck breast rest, off the heat, for 5 minutes; slice; and serve topped with the plum sauce. ❁

Note: You remove the skin because duck breast, per 100g serving, drops from 11g of fat to less than 3g of fat when the skin is removed (data from USDA nutrient database).

Nutrition Facts:
(1 serving =
1 duck breast,
1 tablespoon sauce)

Calories	290
Total Fiber	1g
Total Fat	9g
Total Carbs	14g
Total Protein	36g
Vitamin A	8%
Vitamin C	45%
Calcium	4%
Iron	45%

OSTRICH OPEN-FACED SANDWICH WITH SUNDRIED TOMATOES AND CHIMICHURRI SAUCE

Mix all of the ingredients for the marinade into a bowl. Pour the marinade from the bowl into one large sealable plastic bag. Place the steaks into the bag; close the bag; and lay it flat in the refrigerator to marinate overnight.

Preheat grill to high. Combine and mix all of the ingredients for the chimichurri sauce in a small bowl, and set aside. Place the ostrich steaks on the grill, and mark each side; then turn down heat to medium, and cook until ostrich is medium, about 4–5 minutes on each side (should reach an internal temperature of at least 150°F).

Take the steaks off of the grill, and let them rest for 10 minutes. Slice the ostrich into ½-inch slices. Slice the bread on a bias into eight equal slices, and toast the bread on the grill for about 2 minutes each side.

To assemble the open-face sandwiches, fan the ostrich slices on the toast; sprinkle thin slices of sundried tomatoes over the meat; and finish with a teaspoon of chimichurri sauce. ✳

8 4-ounce ostrich steaks (about ¾ inch thick)

3 sundried tomatoes, sliced thinly

½ small French multigrain baguette
    (sliced into 8 thin, even diagonal slices)

MARINADE

2 cups red wine

1 tablespoon finely chopped fresh thyme

2 tablespoons finely chopped garlic

1 tablespoon chopped rosemary leaves

2 tablespoons olive oil

1 teaspoon salt

1 teaspoon black pepper

CHIMICHURRI SAUCE

½ white onion, chopped finely

1 bunch cilantro leaves, chopped finely

2 limes, juiced

Salt and pepper to taste

One quick and easy way to lower calories and carbs is to serve over a salad instead of bread. Note that, at 23g of protein with only 4g of fat, ostrich is an extremely lean meat!

Nutrition Facts: (1 serving = 4 ounces of ostrich, 1 piece of bread, 1 teaspoon of chimichurri)

Calories	220
Total Fiber	2g
Total Fat	4g
Total Carbs	22g
Total Protein	23g
Vitamin A	0%
Vitamin C	10%
Calcium	2%
Iron	30%

Note: Ostrich meat is leaner than almost any meat you will cook, so be sure not to overcook it. Although ostrich is a bird, its taste and texture are much more similar to those of beef. It is higher in iron than beef, so it is very red in color, even when properly cooked.

4 Servings • Prep: 15–20 min. • Marinate: 30 min. (slaw) 15–60 min. (meat)
• Grill: 15–20 min. (until internal temp. is about 150°F) • Rest: 5 min.

109

OSTRICH WITH JICAMA SLAW

1½ pounds ostrich thigh fan

½ cup brown-rice vinegar

1 tablespoon olive or canola oil

2 cloves garlic, minced

2 tablespoons chili powder

2 tablespoons paprika

1 tablespoon ground cumin

Salt and pepper to taste

Cooking spray as needed

JICAMA SLAW

1 small jicama, peeled and thinly sliced

½ small cabbage head, thinly sliced

2 carrots, shredded or thinly sliced

1 small red onion, thinly sliced

½ cup finely chopped cilantro

1–2 limes, juiced

2 tablespoons rice vinegar

2 tablespoons olive or canola oil

Salt and pepper to taste

Mix the vinegar, oil, garlic, chili, paprika, cumin, salt, and pepper together in a bowl. Pour this over the ostrich fan, and let it marinate for 15 minutes to 1 hour.

In a separate bowl, add all of the slaw ingredients, and let it sit for at least 30 minutes.

Preheat grill to high. Sear the meat just until you have marked both sides with grill marks; then turn down the heat to medium or low and continue to cook to desired doneness. (For medium, it should reach an internal temperature of 150°F.) Let the fan rest for at least 5 minutes, off the heat; then slice and serve, topped with the jicama slaw. ✳

This is a full meal, with lots of fiber, and you have dessert!

NUTRITION 4-1-1: INTRODUCING JICAMA

Jicama is low in sodium and high in potassium and fiber, and comes in at just 23 calories for ½ cup. Most people say that jicama is a cross between an apple and a potato because of its slightly sweet taste and crunchy texture (almost like water chestnuts). You can enjoy jicama raw or cooked, but peel it first; the tan skin is inedible. It's great in salads and slaw; I also like to use it sliced for dipping. Fun Fact: Jicama is considered part of the legume family; it is also known as the yam bean.

Nutrition Facts: (1 serving = 6 ounces of ostrich, ¾–1 cup jicama slaw)				
	Calories	430	Vitamin A	150%
	Total Fiber	11g	Vitamin C	100%
	Total Fat	17g	Calcium	10%
	Total Carbs	30g	Iron	60%
	Total Protein	41g		

6 Meat

Red meat has gotten a bad rap. That's right. As a nutritionist, I am putting that out there. I will see women and men who avoid red meat at all cost but will eat a candy bar, chocolate snack cake, or bioengineered sports bar as a snack, all of which have more fat and saturated fat than 3 ounces of lean beef!

	Calories	Fat (g)	Saturated Fat (g)	Protein (g)
Met Rx Big 100 Bar	410	13	7	31
Ring Dings (2)	330	17	12	2
Snickers, 2.1-oz. bar	280	14	5	4
McDonalds cheeseburger	300	12	6	15
Filet mignon (or eye of round), 3 oz.	177	8	3	24
Chicken breast, (3 oz.)	138	3	0	24

112 Cervana Venison Medallions with Pancetta, Toasted-Fennel-Seed Crust, Grilled Summer Vegetables, and Walnut Pesto, Chef Graham Brown

114 Grilled Cervana Venison Chops

115 Coffee-Mole-Rubbed Filet Mignon

116 Balsamic-Glazed Cervana Kebabs with Sweet Peppers, Cipollini Onions, and Fennel Slaw

117 Sirloin Carnitas with Chili-Lime Sour Cream

118 Filet Mignon with Red-Grape Sauce

119 Flatiron Steak with Creamy Horseradish Sauce

120 Skirt Steak with Pepper Chimichurri Sauce

121 Asian-Style BBQ Pork Tenderloin

122 Grilled Pork with Avocado Salsa

123 Philippine-Inspired Pork Lettuce Wraps

124 Arugula-and-Roquefort-Stuffed Grilled Pork Chops

125 Rack of Lamb with Sour Red-Pepper Jelly

126 Wasabi-Spice Rack of Lamb

127 Bison Sirloin Tip with Garlic-Balsamic Beet Sauce

NUTRITION 4-1-1: GRASS-FED VS. CORN-FED

Allowing cows to feed on their natural diet of grass produces a steak that is lower in calories and higher in omega-3 fats and antioxidants than its corn-fed counterpart.

Portion and selection are key when it comes to choosing what to eat. A 16-ounce prime rib from Outback Steakhouse comes in at a whopping 951 calories, 45 grams of fat, and 125 grams of protein. The "Flatiron Steak with Creamy Horseradish Sauce" (4.5 oz) provides 240 calories and 12 grams of total fat, the latter of which can fit into even a 1,500-calorie meal plan; 45 grams of fat from one entrée cannot!

The benefits of red meat include providing a rich source of zinc and heme iron, absorbed easily by the body and particularly important for growing children and active women during childbearing years, who are more prone to iron deficiency. As we age, and sarcopenia (a loss of muscle mass) occurs, consuming nutrient-rich foods and adequate protein is that much more essential. Red meat also provides vitamins B12, B6, B1, chromium, and vitamin K.

Red meat three times a day? No way. Small portions of lean red meat twice a week? Yes, that can work. Additionally, try some foods outside your comfort zone and popular fare. When I was working with the NY Giants Football team, I learned about Cervena, farm-raised venison from New Zealand. Because the venison is farm raised, there is no gamey taste. Instead, these grass-fed, open-range animals produce very lean red meat—providing all of the benefits of micronutrients (vitamins and minerals) but with a much healthier fat profile. I loved it. The players loved it. And so have all my clients who have since tried it. Cervena is a bit more expensive, so may not be your everyday choice, but for a special family meal or event, it is a great way to go. Bison is another game meat that comes in extremely lean with a healthier nutrient profile than many beef cuts. If you have yet to try it, this is your time.

Glance at the chart below. If you are already a meat eater, you may find certain cuts and styles of preparation a healthier, skinnier way to go. If you have been avoiding red meat, you may find that giving meat a chance again in your diet will expand your choices and add some variety.

	Food Item (3 oz. portion)	Calories	Protein (g)	Total Fat (g)	Saturated Fat (g)	Iron (mg)	Zinc (mg)
Beef	Bottom round roast	185	22	10	4	1.8	3.8
	Brisket	246	24	16	6	2.1	5.7
	Eye of round roast	177	24	8	3	1.9	4
	Filet mignon (tenderloin)	275	20	21	8	2.6	3.4
	Sirloin steak	207	23	12	5	1.5	4.1
	Flank steak (skirt steak)	165	24	6	3	1.5	4.2
	Ground beef, 95% lean	145	22	6	3	2.4	5.5
	Ground beef, 80% lean	218	22	13	5	2.5	5.6
	Ground beef, 70% lean	230	22	15	6	2.1	5.1
	New York strip	224	22	14	6	1.4	4
	Pot roast	257	25	16	6	2.2	5.9
	Rib eye	175	25	8	3	1.7	4.7
	Ribs	302	20	24	10	2	5
	Top round steak	202	29	9	3	2.7	3.7
Bison	Ground	152	22	7	3	2.7	4.5
	Top round steak	148	26	4	2	3	3.2
	Rib eye	150	25	4.8	2.1	2.4	2.7
Venison	Venison – ground	159	22	7	3	2.8	4.4
	Venison – top round steak	139	27	2	1	3.6	3.1

8 Servings • Prep: 20–25 min. • Stand/Suffuse: 30 min. • Grill: 7 min.

CERVENA VENISON MEDALLIONS WITH PANCETTA, TOASTED-FENNEL-SEED CRUST, GRILLED SUMMER VEGETABLES, AND WALNUT PESTO

8 3-ounce medallions of Cervena venison

8 thin strips of pancetta or Parma ham

1 tablespoon toasted fennel seeds

Flake salt and cracked pepper to taste

2 tablespoons olive oil

2–3 cloves garlic, chopped

Fresh basil, oregano, and thyme sprigs

Selection of available vegetables such as zucchini, aubergine, capsicum, asparagus, beans, red onion, corn, flat mushrooms, small artichoke hearts, or young fennel bulb.

8 bamboo skewers

WALNUT PESTO

½ cup fresh walnuts

1 small clove garlic, crushed

2 cups flat-leaf parsley leaves

¼ cup walnut oil

¼ cup extra-virgin olive oil

1½ tablespoons fresh cream

Salt and pepper to taste

Grind the fennel seed, salt, and pepper in a mortar and pestle, and rub the mixture into the venison. Allow to stand for ½ hour.

For the pesto, purée the nuts, parsley, and garlic to a paste. Add the oils slowly, and finish with the cream. Season the pesto to your taste.

Preheat grill to high. Chop the vegetables into bite-size pieces, and coat them generously with olive oil and chopped garlic. Add a few small sprigs of basil, oregano, and thyme, and cook them in a grill basket until just al dente.

While the vegetables are cooking, wrap each medallion with a strip of pancetta or Parma ham, and skewer the medallions in pairs onto two skewers at a time. This helps with handling on the grill. Quickly sear the venison on high heat; then remove it to the internal rack if the grill has a hood or to the side away from high heat, and cook for a further 5 minutes. Rest for a few minutes before serving. Venison should be served rare.

Serve the medallions on top of the vegetables with 1 tablespoon of walnut pesto on each medallion. ✿

As Executive Chef, Cervena of New Zealand, Chef Graham Brown is recognized internationally as a leading culinary arts innovator. Chef Graham travels the world educating chefs and consumers through demonstrations at the finest culinary schools, food shows, and professional culinary events. During his more than 40 years as a chef, Chef Graham has won numerous international awards, including gold and silver medals as captain of Team New Zealand in the 1987 World Culinary Arts Festival in Vancouver, Canada, and Gold again at the IKAHOGA in Frankfurt, Germany, in 1988. In addition, he was awarded Chef of the Nation in 1989, and his restaurant Scarborough Fare has received numerous awards.

Personal Wellness: When I'm not traveling, I enjoy the quiet of country life, working my 25-acre deer farm on the outskirts of Christchurch, New Zealand, and restoring and racing vintage motorcycles. I also operate The Cookhouse, a cooking school that teaches small groups how to cook. The classes feature wine and food tours that highlight local produce.

Nutrition Facts: (1 serving = 3-ounce venison medallion, 1 tablespoon of pesto)			
Calories	340	Vitamin A	25%
Total Fiber	3g	Vitamin C	5%
Total Fat	26g	Calcium	4%
Total Carbs	2.5g	Iron	25%
Total Protein	24g		

4 Servings • Prep: 10 min. • Grill: 5 min. (until internal temp. is 180°F)

GRILLED CERVENA VENISON CHOPS

1 8-rib rack of Cervena venison
2 tablespoons vegetable oil
Salt and pepper

Preheat grill to high. Remove the outside silver skin using a sharp knife, and season the meat well. Cut the rack into four double culets, or cook it as a whole piece. Either way, first sear the venison over high heat to get a nice browning. Remove the whole venison rack to the internal cooking rack in the grill hood or to indirect heat, and cook for 35 minutes, or cook the double chops for 10 minutes over medium heat.

Slice the venison into individual chops, and serve with your favorite fresh tomato salsa or tomato chutney. ✸

Nutrition Facts:
(1 serving = 2 ribs)

Calories	280
Total Fiber	0g
Total Fat	12g
Total Carbs	0g
Total Protein	41g
Vitamin A	2%
Vitamin C	0%
Calcium	2%
Iron	35%

If you're serving up sliders, chicken, fish, etc., with venison chops, go for one instead of two; to manage your calories and portions. If it is your only entrée, then pair with a starch or vegetable side.

COFFEE-MOLE-RUBBED FILET MIGNON

4 4-ounce filet mignon medallions

2 tablespoons canola oil

1 tablespoon instant coffee or finely ground espresso

1 teaspoon unsweetened cocoa powder

1 teaspoon ground chipotle pepper

⅛ teaspoon ground cinnamon

1 teaspoon mustard powder

3 tablespoons finely ground dates

½ tablespoon salt

½ tablespoon freshly ground black pepper

Bring the filet mignon medallions to room temperature before cooking to ensure more-consistent cooking throughout the steak and less grilling time.

Preheat grill to high. Combine all of the ingredients except the medallions and oil in a small bowl. Brush 1 tablespoon of the oil onto the medallions; leave the other tablespoon to brush onto grill (to prevent meat from sticking). Rub about 1½–2 tablespoons of the coffee mole onto each steak. Before putting the medallions onto the grill, brush the remaining oil on the section of the grill you will be using.

Place the medallions on the grill over direct heat. Rotate them after 2 minutes (for nice grill marks). After a total of 5 minutes, gently flip the medallions over to the other side. Rotate after 2 minutes, and grill for a total of 5 minutes. (The filets should be medium rare to medium; grill about 2–3 minutes longer on each side for medium well to well done.)

Take the medallions off of the grill, and set aside to let rest for 5–10 minutes before serving. ❁

6

MEAT

NUTRITION 4-1-1: COFFEE BENEFITS
Research shows that coffee drinkers are less likely to develop certain cancers, strokes, Parkinson's disease, and type 2 diabetes. This healthful beverage can also double as a delicious marinade.

Nutrition Facts: (1 serving = 4-ounce medallion)	
Calories	310
Total Fiber	1g
Total Fat	16g
Total Carbs	7g
Total Protein	33g
Vitamin A	0%
Vitamin C	0%
Calcium	2%
Iron	15%

6 Servings • Prep: 25–30 min. • Soak skewers: overnight • Refrigerate: 1 hr.
• Marinate: 3 hrs. to overnight • Grill: 5–7 min.

BALSAMIC-GLAZED CERVENA KEBABS WITH SWEET PEPPERS, CIPOLLINI ONIONS, AND FENNEL SLAW

Combine all of the glaze ingredients well. Refrigerate the glaze until you need it.

Assemble the kebabs by alternating Cervena and vegetables to produce a colorful pattern. (If you use bamboo skewers, presoak them in water overnight. Just before you will use them, remove them and pat them dry.) Marinate the kebabs in the glaze for at least 3 to 4 hours or overnight (but not to exceed 24 hours).

Combine all of the slaw ingredients in a stainless-steel bowl, and mix them well. Refrigerate for at least 1 hour to allow the flavors to combine.

Preheat grill to high. Mist the kebabs with cooking spray to prevent sticking, and place them on the grill, creating grill marks and cooking on all sides until meat is medium rare, approximately 5–7 minutes. While the kebabs are grilling, season them well and brush them with additional glaze. Remove the kebabs from the heat, and keep them warm. Evenly mound the slaw onto six large plates, and top each plate with two skewers. ✿

1½-pounds Cervena venison, Denver leg cut, cut into 1-inch cubes
2 dozen cipollini onions, peeled and blanched
2 sweet red peppers, cut into 1-inch squares
2 dozen basil leaves
1 head radicchio, cut into 1-inch cubes
Salt and pepper to taste
12 skewers
Cooking spray as needed

SLAW
1 head Napa cabbage, shaved paper-thin into strips
1 cup peeled and julienned carrots
1 cup strips of fennel shaved paper-thin
½ cup thin strips of red onions
1 teaspoon pulverized fennel seed
2 tablespoons fresh mayonnaise
1 tablespoon sour cream
½ tablespoon honey
2 teaspoons freshly squeezed lemon juice
Salt and pepper to taste

GLAZE
1 cup balsamic vinegar
½ cup maple syrup
¼ cup soy sauce

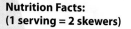

Nutrition Facts: (1 serving = 2 skewers)	
Calories	230
Total Fiber	6g
Total Fat	2.5g
Total Carbs	4g
Total Protein	48g
Vitamin A	120%
Vitamin C	150%
Calcium	15%
Iron	4%

This is a higher protein option and will probably keep you full and satiated for quite a while! If you care to pair it with a nice cabernet, sip and enjoy!

SIRLOIN CARNITAS WITH CHILI-LIME SOUR CREAM

1½ pounds sirloin

1 large red pepper, grilled then sliced

1 large green pepper, grilled then sliced

1 large yellow onion, sliced thick then grilled

8 small corn tortillas

Salt and pepper to taste

CHILI-LIME SOUR CREAM

1 lime, juiced

½ cup fat-free sour cream

¼ teaspoon cumin

Pinch cayenne pepper

1 teaspoon chili powder

¼ teaspoon salt

Preheat grill to high. Season the sirloin with salt and pepper, and grill on both sides to desired doneness, 5–10 minutes per side. At the same time, grill the peppers and onions until grill marks appear. Set the sirloin and vegetables on a baking sheet in a pre-warmed oven to keep warm. Also lightly grill the corn tortillas, just until grill marks appear.

Mix all of the chili-lime sour cream ingredients together in a bowl. Once you have made the sour cream, slice the sirloin against the grain into ½-inch-thick slices, and serve family style. ✿

Recognize that this already has a starchy carbohydrate built into the recipe, which means pairing it with a simple green salad or grilled vegetables is all you need to do to make this meal complete.

Nutrition Facts: (1 serving = 6 ounces of sirloin, 2 tortillas)	
Calories	370
Total Fiber	5g
Total Fat	13g
Total Carbs	27g
Total Protein	34g
Vitamin A	30%
Vitamin C	120%
Calcium	8%
Iron	25%

FILET MIGNON WITH RED-GRAPE SAUCE

4 4-ounce filet mignon medallions

1 tablespoon extra-virgin olive oil
    (to prevent filets from sticking to grill)

Salt and pepper to taste

SAUCE

1 pound seedless red grapes, sliced in half

1 large shallot, diced

2 cups red wine (will reduce by half)

½ teaspoon extra-virgin olive oil

Salt and pepper to taste

Preheat grill to high. Heat ½ teaspoon of oil in a saucepan on the grill to start the grape sauce. Sweat the shallots until they are translucent. Add the halved grapes, and cook until they shrink and reduce by one-half. Add the red wine, and cook until the mixture reduces by one-half and has the consistency of syrup. Take the saucepan off the grill, and let the grape sauce cool down for 10 minutes.

Season the filet medallions with olive oil, salt, and pepper. Grill them 5–8 minutes on each side to desired doneness. Remove the filets from the grill; pour the sauce over them; and serve. ✻

NUTRITION 4-1-1: HEART PROTECTOR

Some studies suggest that whole red grapes offer the same heart-protecting benefits of red wine, with the added benefit of fiber. Just remember, the darker the grape, the higher the antioxidant level.

Nutrition Facts: (1 serving = 4-ounce medallion, 1–2 tablespoons of sauce)

Calories	230
Total Fiber	0g
Total Fat	9g
Total Carbs	1g
Total Protein	32g
Vitamin A	0%
Vitamin C	0%
Calcium	2%
Iron	10%

FLATIRON STEAK WITH CREAMY HORSERADISH SAUCE

4 4–5-ounce beef flatiron steaks, fat trimmed

Salt and pepper to taste

Cooking spray as needed

SAUCE

1 teaspoon finely chopped roasted shallots

1 tablespoon Greek yogurt

1 tablespoon low-fat mayonnaise

2 teaspoons prepared horseradish

Salt and pepper to taste

Preheat grill to high. Season the steak with salt and pepper, and mist it lightly with the cooking spray. Sear the steak, marking both sides, for a minute or two per side. Turn down the heat to medium, and finish cooking to desired doneness. Remove the steak from the heat, and let it rest for a minimum of 5 minutes.

As the meat rests, mix all of the sauce ingredients together in a bowl, and whisk thoroughly. Slice the steak, and add a dollop of the horseradish sauce when you serve it. ❋

6

MEAT

NUTRITION 4-1-1: CANCER FIGHTER

Studies show that the high levels of glucosinolates found in horseradish may increase resistance to cancer, and because it is so potent, the effective dose may be as small as 1 gram.

Nutrition Facts:
(1 serving = 1 steak,
½–¾ tablespoon of sauce)

Calories	240
Total Fiber	0g
Total Fat	12g
Total Carbs	1g
Total Protein	32g
Vitamin A	0%
Vitamin C	2%
Calcium	2%
Iron	20%

SKIRT STEAK WITH PEPPER CHIMICHURRI SAUCE

1 pound skirt steak, fat trimmed

1 tablespoon extra-virgin olive oil
   (to prevent filets from sticking to grill)

Salt and pepper to taste

SAUCE/MARINADE

½ cup parsley or cilantro

⅓ cup oregano

3 cloves garlic, minced

1 tablespoon minced shallots

½ cup extra-virgin olive oil

Juice and zest of 1 lemon

Salt and pepper to taste

½ cup finely diced bell peppers
   (tri-colored if possible)

Gather all of the ingredients for the sauce/marinade, except the peppers, and purée them in a blender on high. Pour the mixture into a bowl, and add the diced peppers. Marinate the steak in the sauce overnight, making sure you reserve ¼ cup to apply to the steak after cooking.

Preheat grill to high. Brush the meat with the oil, and season it with the salt and pepper. Sear the steak, marking both sides, for a minute or so per side. Turn down the heat to medium, and finish cooking to desired doneness.

Remove the steak from the heat, and let it rest for a minimum of 5 minutes.

Slice the steak against the grain, and top each serving with 1 teaspoon of reserved Chimichurri sauce. ✿

Note: Shown family style, not portioned.

Nutrition Facts: (1 serving = 4 ounces of skirt steak, 1 teaspoon of sauce)

Calories	230
Total Fiber	1g
Total Fat	14g
Total Carbs	1g
Total Protein	24g
Vitamin A	0%
Vitamin C	10%
Calcium	2%
Iron	15%

NUTRITION 4-1-1: MEDICINAL CILANTRO
Cilantro has been used for many years, not only for cooking but for medicinal purposes as well. Cilantro may be used to treat urinary tract infections, nausea, rheumatic pain, headaches, coughs, and mental stress; relieve intestinal gas; aid in digestion; and soothe inflammation. Fun Fact: Cilantro is a member of the carrot family.

4 Servings • Prep: 10–15 min. • Marinate: 1 hr. to overnight • Grill: 20–26 min. (until internal temp. is at least 145°F) • Rest: 5 min.

ASIAN-STYLE BBQ PORK TENDERLOIN

¾–1 pound pork tenderloin, fat trimmed
Juice and zest of 1 orange
¼ cup low-sodium soy sauce
¼ cup brown-rice vinegar
¼ cup dark-brown sugar
2 tablespoons grated ginger
1 clove garlic, minced
1 tablespoon sambal oelek chili sauce
½ cup chopped cilantro
Carrot shavings and/or thinly sliced red pepper (optional garnish)
Cooking spray as needed

Combine the orange juice and zest, soy sauce, vinegar, sugar, ginger, garlic, and chili sauce in a bowl. Put the pork and the marinade you just made in a sealable plastic bag, and marinate for 1 hour to overnight.

Preheat grill to high. Mist the pork with the cooking spray to prevent sticking. Sear the pork on all sides; then lower the heat to medium, and cook the meat to an internal temperature of at least 145°F or more, according to taste. Remove the tenderloin from the heat, and let it rest for a minimum of 5 minutes. Slice and serve, garnished with the fresh cilantro and/or carrot shavings and thin-sliced pepper.

Nutrition Facts:
(1 serving = 3–4 ounces of pork tenderloin)

Calories	240
Total Fiber	1g
Total Fat	4.5g
Total Carbs	23g
Total Protein	25g
Vitamin A	2%
Vitamin C	30%
Calcium	2%
Iron	8%

4 Servings • Prep: 20–25 min.
• Grill: 14–20 min. (until internal temp. is at least 145°F) • Rest: 5 min.

GRILLED PORK WITH AVOCADO SALSA

¾–1 pound boneless top-loin pork chops, thick
    cut (or pork tenderloin if unavailable)

½ cup rough-chopped Spanish onions

½ cup freshly squeezed lime juice

2 tablespoons extra-virgin olive oil

¼ cup seeded and chopped jalapeño peppers

2 teaspoons freshly ground cumin

1 teaspoon salt

1 teaspoon freshly ground black pepper

Water as needed

SALSA

1 Hass avocado, peeled, pit removed, and medium diced

1 cup halved cherry or pear tomatoes

½ cup seeded and medium-diced cucumber

¼ cup finely diced red onion

¼ cup chopped cilantro

1 tablespoon extra-virgin olive oil

1–2 tablespoons freshly squeezed lime juice

Salt and pepper to taste

Create a marinade by combining the Spanish onions, ½ cup of lime juice, 2 tablespoons of oil, jalapeño, cumin, and 1 teaspoon each of salt and pepper in a blender and blending on high until smooth. If the marinade does not blend properly, add water, a little at a time, until the mixture purées. Put the pork and the marinade in a sealable plastic bag, and marinate for 1 hour to overnight.

Preheat grill to high. Mix all of the salsa ingredients together in a bowl close to the time you will serve the dish to prevent browning (enzymatic oxidation) of the avocado. Mist the pork with the cooking spray to prevent sticking. Sear the pork on all sides; then lower the heat to medium, and cook the meat to an internal temperature of at least 145°F or more, according to taste. Remove the tenderloin from the heat, and let it rest for a minimum of 5 minutes. Slice and serve with a generous serving of the salsa. ✳

Nutrition Facts: Pork
(1 serving = 3-4 ounces of pork chop)

Calories	160
Total Fiber	0g
Total Fat	7g
Total Carbs	0g
Total Protein	24g
Vitamin A	0%
Vitamin C	0%
Calcium	4%
Iron	4%

Nutrition Facts: Avocado salsa
(1 serving = 1 tablespoon)

Calories	190
Total Fiber	1g
Total Fat	16g
Total Carbs	11g
Total Protein	2g
Vitamin A	8%
Vitamin C	40%
Calcium	4%
Iron	4%

4 Servings • Prep: 25–30 min.
• Grill: 20–26 min. (until internal temp. is at least 145°F) • Rest: 10 min.

123

PHILIPPINE-INSPIRED PORK LETTUCE WRAPS

½–¾ pound pork loin roast, fat trimmed

1 onion, finely diced

1 red bell pepper, finely diced

2 cloves garlic, minced

1 cup cooked brown rice, cooled overnight

½ cup chopped cilantro

1 jalapeño pepper, seeded and chopped

1 tablespoon extra-virgin olive oil

½ cup brown-rice vinegar

Salt and pepper to taste

Cooking spray as needed

1 Boston bibb or iceberg lettuce

1 lime, wedged

Preheat grill to high. Mist the pork with the cooking spray to prevent sticking, and season it with the salt and pepper. Sear the pork on all sides; then lower the heat to medium or low, and cook the roast to an internal temperature of at least 145°F or more, according to taste. Remove the tenderloin from the heat, and let it rest for at least 10 minutes.

Chop the pork into ¼-to-½-inch cubes, and add them to a bowl. Add all of the other ingredients, reserving the lettuce as a wrap. Place a generous spoonful of the mixture into a lettuce leaf, and serve with a lime wedge. ✦

6

MEAT

This is another complete meal unto itself, with the rice mixed in with the meat. Add some appetizers or a dessert because you have another 250 calories left for the meal.

Nutrition Facts: (1 serving = 2–3 ounces pork loin, or 2–3 lettuce wraps)

Calories	240
Total Fiber	3g
Total Fat	7g
Total Carbs	23g
Total Protein	20g
Vitamin A	45%
Vitamin C	90%
Calcium	4%
Iron	10%

4 Servings • Prep: 15–20 min.
• Grill: 14–20 min. (until internal temp. is at least 145°F) • Rest: 5–10 min.

ARUGULA-AND-ROQUEFORT-STUFFED PORK CHOPS

4 4–5-ounce boneless pork chops

2 cups chopped baby arugula

½ cup julienned red onion

¼ cup Roquefort or other blue cheese

1 Bosc pear, diced small

¼ cup roasted pine nuts

2 tablespoons olive oil

Salt and pepper to taste

1 teaspoon fresh lemon juice

Cooking spray as needed

Gently mix the arugula, onion, cheese, pear, nuts, and olive oil in a bowl. Adjust the seasonings.

Using a paring knife, create a pocket in the pork chops by inserting the knife into the side of the chop and working around the interior, making sure not to pierce the edges. Using your fingers, stuff the chops with the arugula mixture.

Preheat grill to high. Mist the stuffed chops with the cooking spray to prevent sticking, and season the top each one with salt and pepper. Sear the chops on both sides to create grill marks; then lower the heat to medium or low, and cook them to an internal temperature of at least 145°F or more, according to taste. Remove the chops from the heat, and let them rest for 5–10 minutes. Cut each chop into thick slices, and serve topped with a squeeze of lemon juice. ❋

This is a big-flavor entrée, and though it's on the high side of fat and calories, compared with some traditional meat-and-cheese combos, this is a caloric saver.

Nutrition Facts: (1 serving = 1 stuffed pork chop)	
Calories	380
Total Fiber	5g
Total Fat	23g
Total Carbs	9g
Total Protein	34g
Vitamin A	8%
Vitamin C	8%
Calcium	15%
Iron	8%

RACK OF LAMB WITH SOUR RED-PEPPER JELLY

You should make the jelly a day before you plan to serve the dish. To do so, heat a saucepan over medium heat, and sauté the peppers in 1 tablespoon of oil until the peppers become soft. Add the sugar and vinegar, and reduce the liquid by one-half. Stir in the pectin, salt, pepper, and if desired, red-pepper flakes and mint. Transfer the liquid to a bowl, and allow to cool overnight in the refrigerator.

Preheat grill to high. Remove any excess fat from the rib rack after Frenching it; season with the other tablespoon of oil, salt, and pepper; and generously coat with mustard. Grill to desired doneness, 7 minutes or more a side, and set aside to rest for at least 5 minutes.

Cut the rack apart, serving two-rib portions topped with a tablespoon of the pepper jelly. ✽

1 8-rib rack of lamb, Frenched and
    fat cap trimmed
2 tablespoons extra-virgin olive oil
¼ cup Dijon mustard
Salt and pepper to taste

RED-PEPPER JELLY
½ pound red bell peppers, small diced
1 tablespoon extra-virgin olive oil
1½ cups sugar
½ cup brown-rice vinegar
4 ounces liquid pectin
1 teaspoon salt
½ teaspoon freshly ground black pepper
1 teaspoon dried hot red-pepper flakes (optional)
1 tablespoon chopped fresh mint (optional)

6

MEAT

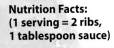

Nutrition Facts: (1 serving = 2 ribs, 1 tablespoon sauce)	
Calories	280
Total Fiber	0g
Total Fat	18g
Total Carbs	5g
Total Protein	23g
Vitamin A	2%
Vitamin C	10%
Calcium	2%
Iron	10%

4 Servings • Prep: min. • Grill: 14–20 min. • Rest: 5 min.

WASABI-SPICE RACK OF LAMB

1 8-rib rack of lamb, Frenched and fat cap trimmed

1 tablespoon kosher salt

1 tablespoon whole pink peppercorns

1 tablespoon whole black peppercorns

1 tablespoon whole coriander

½ –1 tablespoon wasabi powder

1 teaspoon ginger powder

¼ cup Dijon mustard

¼ cup sweet mirin rice wine

2 tablespoons extra-virgin olive oil or canola oil

Cooking spray as needed

Grind the salt, peppercorns, coriander, wasabi, and ginger together in a spice grinder or coffee grinder. Mix the mustard, mirin, and oil together in a bowl until blended. Add the spice mixture to the mustard mixture, and set aside.

Preheat grill to high. Remove any excess fat from the rib rack after Frenching it; mist it with cooking spray to prevent sticking; and sear it, being mindful not to burn the bones too much, until it is well marked on the outside. When the rack is seared, reduce the heat and generously brush it with the wasabi-spice mixture. Continue to grill and baste the rack until it reaches your desired internal temperature, about 140°F to 150°F for medium.

Let the rack rest for at least 5 minutes before cutting it apart, and serve two ribs per serving. ✸

Nutrition Facts:
(1 serving = ¼ lamb rack)

Calories	410
Total Fiber	1g
Total Fat	21g
Total Carbs	14g
Total Protein	24g
Vitamin A	0%
Vitamin C	0%
Calcium	4%
Iron	20%

BISON SIRLOIN TIP WITH GARLIC-BALSAMIC BEET SAUCE

1 pound bison top sirloin tip

2 tablespoons olive or canola oil

1 cup balsamic vinegar

1 cup beet juice (note below)

2 tablespoons extra-virgin olive oil

2 cloves garlic, roasted

1 teaspoon Dijon mustard
   (optional, but it will improve texture)

1 tablespoon picked-and-rough-chopped
   fresh rosemary

2 tablespoons fresh lemon juice

Salt and pepper to taste

Note: Beet juice can be difficult to find, and juicers are expensive. You can substitute one roasted beet and ¾–1 cup of water or beef stock, puréed smooth in a blender, for conventional beet juice. Depending on the size of the beet, this may make your sauce thicker than desired. Have some extra water or beef stock on hand to help you adjust the texture.

Preheat grill to high. Rub the sirloin tip with 2 tablespoons of oil, salt, and pepper, and set it aside. Now heat the balsamic vinegar in a saucepan on the grill, and reduce it by one-half. Add the beet juice, and reduce that mixture by one-quarter. Set the reduction aside to cool to room temperature.

Sear the bison tip on each side for 2 minutes, rotating it after 1 minute to create diamond grill marks. Reduce the heat to medium, and grill the bison to your desired doneness (155°F for medium). Once it's done, set it aside to rest for at least 5 minutes.

Combine the beet-balsamic reduction, extra-virgin olive oil, garlic, mustard (optional), rosemary, lemon, salt, and pepper in a blender, and purée until smooth. (If the rosemary doesn't completely blend into the sauce, consider straining the sauce before serving it.)

Cut the sirloin tip into thin slices, and top each serving with 1–2 tablespoons of the balsamic beet sauce. ✸

6

MEAT

Nutrition Facts: (1 serving = 4 ounces of bison, 2 tablespoons of sauce)	
Calories	310
Total Fiber	1g
Total Fat	16g
Total Carbs	7g
Total Protein	33g
Vitamin A	0%
Vitamin C	0%
Calcium	2%
Iron	15%

Game meats may or may not be easy to find depending on where you live. Many specialty meat retailers will stock a wide variety. You can always find and buy on-line from Web sites such as www.cervena.com. One place our photographer, Glen Teitell, came across is FossilFarms.com. He was "overjoyed to find a place that carries all the less-than-pedestrian meats, all under one roof!" Another option: www.dartagnan.com.

7 Burgers & Sliders

According to "The New (Ab)Normal" (makinghealtheasir.org), the average size of a burger, since the 1950s, has increased by 223%! Adults, on average, are 26 pounds heavier as well. So perhaps it's not the burger but its size that's the problem.

130 Tuna Slider with Wasabi Spread, Chef Todd Seyfarth

132 Teriyaki Chicken Slider

133 Turkey-Cranberry Slider with Green Bean Pesto

134 Mustard-and-Mint Ground Lamb with Feta-Yogurt Sauce

135 Lean Ground Pork with Asian Slaw

136 Cervena Venison Sliders with Three Toppings

138 Salmon Slider

139 Ultimate Portobello Slider

140 Vegetarian Lentil Slider

141 Jerk Bison Slider with Fruit Salsa

Better Burgers, Smarter Sliders

Any of the recipes in this section can be made larger or smaller, based on your mood, taste preference, and caloric needs. Sometimes, you just want to bite into two sides of a bun and eat a good old burger. If you are enjoying many options at a barbecue, you may want to go to a smaller slider portion, which is what we show here in *Grill Yourself Skinny*. If you are eating several side dishes, you may want to skip the bun all together or try an open-faced burger. I sometimes use the bottom half of the bun and a great lettuce leaf folded over as the top.

Adding vegetables to ground meat adds taste, fiber, and healthy ingredients, and it lowers the amount of meat needed. Of course, not all sliders are meat. In this section you will find salmon, tuna, lentil, and portobello mushroom, as well as turkey, chicken, Cervena venison, bison, lamb, and pork, in addition to traditional ground beef.

When you add vegetables, they add moisture, so it is a delicate balance between just right and too much—where your slider falls apart. Try using ½ cup of puréed vegetables to each pound of ground meat as a guideline. You can use whatever vegetables you like: mushroom adds an "unami" experience and most closely matches meat texture; root vegetables work as well. Carrots add some sweetness. If you use greens like spinach, just be sure to drain them well. Really, any vegetable will work. By using the food processor to purée, the vegetable mixture blends easily with the meat. When you make the patties, pat gently instead of packing densely.

Binders such as bread crumbs are traditional . . . try 100% whole wheat instead of white, or use instant oatmeal, quinoa, or even beans—just make sure that you have properly drained them to remove any excess moisture. Eggs are also binders because the heat coagulates the egg protein and helps hold the slider together.

Burgers and sliders are a staple for the grill. Hopefully, you will find some wonderful new flavors and favorites in this section.

Analyses for sliders are based without a bun. Sometimes, you just want to bite into a burger with a bun—at other times you might be OK with an open-face slider or lettuce wrap. If you use the bun, be mindful of which other appetizers or sides you choose because you can easily go over on carbohydrates and calories without a lot of additional food.

NUTRITION 4-1-1: WONDERFUL OMEGA-3

Fatty fish, such as tuna, contain the highest levels of omega-3 fatty acids, which have been shown to lower blood pressure, decrease triglycerides, enhance immunity, and alleviate arthritis symptoms. Although fresh tuna has great health benefits, studies state that mercury levels in tuna still remain high, so eat in moderation. Pregnant women and small children should avoid all fish high in mercury; this includes shark, swordfish, mackerel, and tilefish.

TUNA SLIDER WITH WASABI SPREAD

1 pound tuna loin, sushi-grade and fresh

½ cup egg substitute or 2 whole eggs

¼ cup thinly sliced green onions (scallions)

2 tablespoons dark chili power

2 tablespoons low-sodium soy sauce

Whole-wheat bread crumbs, couscous, or instant
    oatmeal as needed

Salt and pepper to taste

Cooking spray as needed

Shredded romaine or iceberg lettuce as needed

Pickled ginger slices as needed

Tomato slices as needed

Red onion slices as needed

Whole-wheat buns, bread, or English muffins
    (optional)

WASABI SPREAD

1–2 tablespoons wasabi powder

½ cup low-fat or fat-free Greek yogurt

1 tablespoon mirin rice wine

Salt and pepper to taste

In a food processor, add the tuna, eggs, green onions, chili powder, soy sauce, salt, and pepper, and "pulse" blend until the ingredients are mixed but not puréed. (The mixture may be very soft and moist at this point.) Transfer to a bowl, and add the binder you choose (bread crumbs, etc.) a little at a time until the mixture becomes malleable and you can form patties. Form the mixture into eight slider-size burgers, and let them rest for 30 minutes to overnight (in the refrigerator).

Combine the wasabi, yogurt, and mirin in a bowl, and whisk until smooth, making sure there are no "wasabi lumps." Season the spread with salt and pepper, and set it aside.

Preheat grill to medium. Lightly mist the sliders with the cooking spray to prevent sticking, and cook them to 145°F internal temperature or desired doneness, 3 to 5 minutes per side. Serve the sliders over shredded lettuce (or a bun, bread, or English muffin) topped with about a tablespoon of the wasabi spread and pickled ginger, tomato, and/or red onion.

Todd Seyfarth is a Chef, Registered Dietitian, and Associate Professor of Culinary Nutrition at Johnson & Wales University. He specializes in high-end, à la carte, nutritional cuisine as well as athletic performance cuisine, holistic approaches to weight management, and spa cuisine. Chef Seyfarth joined the faculty of Johnson & Wales University in 2003, and previously taught at the New York Food and Hotel Management School, in New York City. Prior to that, he had honed his culinary skills working in the Hamptons of Long Island. Chef Seyfarth has presented his philosophy of healthy cooking to elementary school children, to fortune 500 companies, and at various regional and national food and nutrition conferences.

Personal Wellness: As someone who hates the gym and loathes the idea of climbing stairs or running for hours and ending up in the same place, I try to incorporate as much sport into my exercise routine as possible. Bike rides and basketball are favorites. When it comes to eating right, I find that eating simply prepared seasonal foods helps keep me happy and healthy. You can never go wrong with quality over quantity when it comes to your food choices!

Nutrition Facts: (1 serving = 1 slider, without bun, 1 tablespoon spread)			
	Calories	130	Vitamin A	45%
	Total Fiber	1g	Vitamin C	4%
	Total Fat	3.5g	Calcium	4%
	Total Carbs	13g	Iron	8%
	Total Protein	17g		

TERIYAKI CHICKEN SLIDER

1 pound lean ground chicken

½ cup egg substitute or 2 whole eggs

½ cup puréed vegetables (per note below)

½ cup low sodium teriyaki sauce

¼ cup thinly sliced green onions (scallions)

1 tablespoon minced garlic

Whole-wheat bread crumbs, couscous, or instant
   oatmeal as needed

2 heads baby bok choy, spit into quarters lengthwise

2 tablespoons canola or peanut oil

¼ cup brown-rice vinegar

Salt and pepper to taste

Cooking spray as needed

Whole-wheat buns, bread, or English muffins (optional)

Mix the chicken, eggs, vegetable purée, teriyaki, onions, garlic, salt, and pepper in a bowl. (The mixture may be very soft and moist at this point.) Add the desired binder (bread crumbs, etc.) a little at a time until the mixture becomes malleable and you can form patties. Form the mixture into eight slider-size burgers, and let them rest for 30 minutes to overnight (in the refrigerator).

Preheat grill to medium high. Place the quartered bok choy pieces in a bowl, and toss them with the oil, vinegar, salt, and pepper. Lightly mist the sliders with the cooking spray to prevent sticking. Cook the sliders (to at least 165°F internal temperature, about 3 to 5 minutes per side) *and* the bok choy together to desired doneness. Place each slider on your bread of choice (optional), and top it with the bok choy and your favorite burger condiments. ☙

Nutrition Facts:
(1 serving =
1 slider, without bun)

Calories	150
Total Fiber	1g
Total Fat	8g
Total Carbs	7g
Total Protein	13g
Vitamin A	15%
Vitamin C	6%
Calcium	4%
Iron	6%

Note: For the vegetable purée, the kind of vegetable is not really important. The vegetables will mimic some of the properties of the missing fat, giving you a moist, tender product. When considering which vegetable to use, reflect on what is available, what flavors you like on the burgers (mushroom, onion, or wilted spinach, etc.), or what you have leftover in your refrigerator.

TURKEY-CRANBERRY SLIDER WITH GREEN BEAN PESTO

1 pound lean ground turkey

½ cup egg substitute or 2 whole eggs

½ cup puréed vegetables (note on page 132)

½ cup dried cranberries

¼ cup finely chopped celery

2 tablespoons chopped fresh thyme

2 tablespoons chopped fresh rosemary

1 tablespoon chopped fresh sage

Salt and pepper to taste

Whole-wheat bread crumbs, couscous, or instant oatmeal as needed

Cooking spray as needed

Tomato and red onion, sliced, as needed

Romaine or iceberg lettuce as needed

Whole-wheat toast, buns, or English muffins (optional)

In a bowl, mix the turkey, eggs, vegetable purée, cranberries, celery, herbs, salt, and pepper. (The mixture may be very soft and moist at this point.) Add the binder you choose (bread crumbs, etc.) until the mixture becomes malleable and you can form patties. Make eight slider-size burgers, and let them rest for 30 minutes to overnight (in the refrigerator).

Put all of the pesto ingredients, except the water, in a food processor. Pulse for 10–20 seconds. If a chunky paste does not form, add water 1 tablespoon at a time until it does.

Preheat grill to medium high. Mist the sliders lightly with the cooking spray, and cook them to 165°F internal temperature or to your liking. Serve with the pesto, your favorite burger condiments, and toast or a bun if you choose. ◉

7

BURGERS & SLIDERS

GREEN BEAN PESTO

2 ounces green beans, trimmed and blanched

1 clove garlic

1 teaspoon extra-virgin olive oil

1–2 tablespoons water (blanching liquid or tap water) as needed to make mixture smooth

2 tablespoons oregano leaves

¼ cup picked basil leaves

1 tablespoon Parmesan cheese

Salt and pepper to taste

Nutrition Facts:
(1 serving =
1 slider, without bun)

Calories	140
Total Fiber	1g
Total Fat	2g
Total Carbs	13g
Total Protein	17g
Vitamin A	35%
Vitamin C	30%
Calcium	20%
Iron	8%

MUSTARD-AND-MINT GROUND LAMB WITH FETA-YOGURT SAUCE

1 pound lean ground lamb

½ cup egg substitute or 2 whole eggs

½ cup puréed vegetables (note below)

2 tablespoons Dijon mustard

¼ cup chopped fresh mint

¼ cup chopped fresh rosemary

Whole-wheat bread crumbs, couscous, or instant oatmeal as needed

Salt and pepper to taste

Cooking spray as needed

Tomato and red onion, sliced, as needed

Romaine or iceberg lettuce as needed

Whole-wheat buns, bread, or English muffins (optional)

SAUCE

1 cup low-fat or fat-free Greek yogurt

¼ cup crumbled feta cheese

¼ cup grated cucumber

Salt and pepper as needed

First, fold all of the sauce ingredients together in a bowl. Then mix the lamb, eggs, vegetable purée, herbs, salt, and pepper in a separate bowl. (The mixture may be very soft and moist at this point.) Add the desired binder (bread crumbs, etc.) a little at a time until the mixture becomes malleable and you can form patties. Make eight slider-size burgers, and let them rest for 30 minutes to overnight (in the refrigerator).

Preheat grill to medium high. Mist the sliders lightly with the cooking spray to prevent sticking, and cook them for 5–6 minutes per side for medium rare (145°F internal temperature) or to desired doneness. Mix the sauce ingredients together in a small bowl. Place the sliders on toasted buns or another bread of your choice if desired; top them with the yogurt sauce; and serve with your favorite burger condiments. ○

Nutrition Facts:
(1 serving =
1 slider, without bun)

Calories	200
Total Fiber	1g
Total Fat	12g
Total Carbs	4g
Total Protein	17g
Vitamin A	20%
Vitamin C	4%
Calcium	6%
Iron	10%

Note: For the vegetable purée, the kind of vegetable is not really important. The vegetables will mimic some of the properties of the missing fat, giving you a moist, tender product. When considering which vegetable to use, reflect on what is available, what flavors you like on the burgers (mushroom, onion, or wilted spinach, etc.), or what you have leftover in your refrigerator.

LEAN GROUND PORK WITH ASIAN SLAW

1 pound lean ground pork

½ cup egg substitute or 2 whole eggs

½ cup puréed vegetables (note on page 134)

2 tablespoons hoisin sauce

1 tablespoon minced garlic

1 teaspoon minced ginger

Whole-wheat bread crumbs, couscous,
   or instant oatmeal as needed

Salt and pepper to taste

Cooking spray as needed

Whole-wheat English muffins, buns,
   or bread (optional)

SLAW

¼ cup rice wine vinegar

½ cup low-fat or fat-free Greek yogurt

2 tablespoons low-sodium soy sauce

2 cups shredded green, red, or Napa cabbage (or combination)

½ cup shredded carrots

½ cup thinly sliced red onion or green onions (scallions)

1 teaspoon black sesame seeds

Salt and pepper to taste

½ cup chopped fresh cilantro (optional)

Mix the pork, eggs, vegetable purée, hoisin, garlic, ginger, salt, and pepper in a bowl. (The mixture may be very soft and moist at this point.) Add the binder you choose (bread crumbs, etc.) a little at a time until the mixture becomes malleable and you can form patties. Make eight slider-sized burgers, and let them rest for 30 minutes to overnight (in the refrigerator).

Mix the vinegar, yogurt, and soy sauce in a bowl, forming a sauce for the slaw. Add the rest of the slaw ingredients, and let the mixture sit for at least 30 minutes.

Preheat grill to medium high. Lightly mist the sliders with the cooking spray to prevent sticking. Cook the sliders to at least 160°F internal temperature; place them on a toasted English muffin or other bread if you desire; and top them with the slaw and your favorite burger condiments. ✿

NUTRITION 4-1-1: CABBAGE
Cabbage boasts the same health benefits as the other members of the cruciferous vegetable family, with the addition of the cancer-fighting compounds known as indoles.

Nutrition Facts:
(1 serving =
1 slider, without bun)

Calories	180
Total Fiber	1g
Total Fat	2.5g
Total Carbs	16g
Total Protein	22g
Vitamin A	35%
Vitamin C	6%
Calcium	8%
Iron	8%

2 pounds Cervena venison from the leg

1 teaspoon dried oregano

1 teaspoon ground cinnamon

8 stems flat leaf parsley, leaves removed and finely chopped

2 teaspoons extra-virgin olive oil

2 teaspoons Maldon salt (note on page 137)

½ teaspoon freshly ground pepper

Small egg buns or whole-wheat buns, bread, or English muffins (optional)

TOPPING 1: SHERRY VINEGAR ONIONS

1 red onion, peeled and cut into ½-inch rounds

1 bay leaf

1 stem rosemary

½ teaspoon dried oregano

1 clove garlic, flattened with the side of a knife

3½ tablespoons sherry vinegar

3 tablespoons extra-virgin olive oil

1 tablespoon dark-brown sugar

½ tablespoon Maldon or kosher salt

TOPPING 2: SWEET AND SOUR TOMATOES

1-pound can peeled and crushed tomatoes

½ thumb ginger, peeled and finely chopped

3 cloves garlic, minced

2 teaspoons Tabasco sauce

¾ cup sugar

1 tablespoon fish sauce

5 tablespoons cider vinegar

TOPPING 3: PICKLED BEETS

1 pound beetroot

1 red chili, deseeded and finely chopped

5 cloves garlic, finely chopped

1 knob ginger, peeled and finely chopped

¾ cup muscovado or dark-brown sugar

2 cups Greek red wine vinegar

1 cup cider vinegar

Salt and black pepper to taste

4 organic eggs

Nutrition Facts: (1 serving = 1 slider without bun, topping 1)	
Calories	110
Total Fiber	0g
Total Fat	4.5g
Total Carbs	2g
Total Protein	13g
Vitamin A	0%
Vitamin C	2%
Calcium	0%
Iron	10%

Nutrition Facts: (1 serving = 1 slider without bun, topping 2)	
Calories	110
Total Fiber	0g
Total Fat	2g
Total Carbs	10g
Total Protein	14g
Vitamin A	2%
Vitamin C	6%
Calcium	2%
Iron	10%

Nutrition Facts: (1 serving = 1 slider without bun, topping 3)	
Calories	150
Total Fiber	0g
Total Fat	3g
Total Carbs	15g
Total Protein	15g
Vitamin A	2%
Vitamin C	10%
Calcium	2%
Iron	15%

Nutrition Facts: (1 serving = 1 slider without bun, no toppings)	
Calories	70
Total Fiber	0g
Total Fat	2g
Total Carbs	0g
Total Protein	13g
Vitamin A	0%
Vitamin C	0%
Calcium	0%
Iron	10%

CERVENA VENISON SLIDERS WITH THREE TOPPINGS

VENISON COOKING TIPS

Cervena venison is a lean, healthy meat with about one-fifth the fat of beef, so it cooks quickly! Here are some tips to keep the burgers moist:

- If you have a butcher grind the meat, ask him or her to make a course mixture on the largest setting.
- When making the meat into patties, pack them loosely. The texture is more pleasing, and the meat will cook better.
- Use medium heat, and don't cook the burgers past medium (150°F–155°F).

You can make the venison into ground meat in three ways:

- Chop the meat by hand until the pieces are about the size of lentils. Place it in a mixing bowl with the other ingredients and mix until well incorporated (recommended method).
- Roughly chop the meat; place it in a food processor with all of the other ingredients; and lightly pulse the blade until the venison looks like ground meat.
- If you have a meat grinder or the proper attachment to your mixer, mix all of the ingredients together, and push them through the grinder.

Once the meat mixture is ground, separate it into 16 equal portions. Lightly form the meat into slider-size patties, taking care not to pack them too tightly.

Preheat grill to medium. Grill the sliders to medium rare (145°F internal temperature), about 1–2 minutes on each side. Be careful not to overcook the sliders, as the meat cooks very quickly. If desired, use small egg buns, or drizzle olive oil over the buns and grill them to get richer, moister bread.

Topping 1

Preheat an oven to 350°F. Place the onion slices in an even layer in an oven-safe dish. Combine the remaining ingredients in a mixing bowl, and whisk them together. Pour the mixture over the onions.

Cover the oven-safe dish with foil, and place it in the preheated oven for about 40 minutes. The onions will have softened, turned a pale red, and absorbed most of the liquid. Remove the onions from the oven, and allow them to cool. You will end up with more than you need, but they keep well in the refrigerator.

Topping 2

Combine all of the ingredients in a saucepan, and place the pan on medium heat. Bring the sauce to a boil, and reduce the heat to a simmer. Cook the sauce on a low simmer for 30 minutes or until it becomes thick and glossy. Remove the sauce from the heat, and allow it to cool. This also keeps very well in the refrigerator.

Topping 3

Preheat the oven to 375°F. Wash the beets, and wrap them in aluminum foil. Place the foil-wrapped beets on a baking tray, and place it in the oven for about 40–60 minutes, depending on size, or until you can easily insert and remove a sharp knife.

Allow the beets to cool; peel them; and cut them into thin slices. Combine all of the remaining ingredients in a saucepan. Place the pan over medium heat, and bring the contents to a boil. Reduce the heat to a medium simmer, and continue to cook until the volume of liquid is reduced by about one-quarter. Pour the liquid over the sliced beets, and refrigerate. ✪

Note: Maldon salt is a flavorful salt from the UK that you can find in specialty stores, but you can also use kosher salt.

SALMON SLIDER

1 pound salmon fillet

½ cup egg substitute or 2 whole eggs

¼ cup smoothly puréed roasted fennel

¼ cup Dijon mustard

¼ cup thinly sliced chives or green onions (scallions)

2 tablespoons dark chili powder

Salt and pepper to taste

Whole-wheat bread crumbs, couscous, or instant
    oatmeal as needed

Cooking spray as needed

Tomato and red onion, sliced, as needed

Romaine or iceberg lettuce as needed

Whole-wheat buns, bread, or English muffins
    (optional)

*Note: These burgers will be very soft. If the burgers aren't
holding together on the grill, place a piece of aluminum foil
on the grill, and cook them on that. As the sliders begin to
"set," transfer them off of the foil to finish cooking.*

Place the salmon, eggs, fennel, mustard, chives, chili powder, salt, and pepper in a food processor, and "pulse" blend until mixed but not puréed. (The mixture may be very soft and moist at this point.) Transfer the mixture to a bowl, and add the binder you choose (bread crumbs, etc.) a little at a time until the mixture becomes malleable and you can form patties. Make eight slider-size burgers, and let them rest for 30 minutes to overnight (in a refrigerator).

Preheat grill to medium high. Lightly mist the sliders with the cooking spray to prevent sticking. Cook the sliders to 145°F internal temperature or desired doneness. Place the sliders on toasted buns or your bread of choice, and serve with your favorite burger condiments. ✿

Grill-top Tomato and Parmesan, page 150

Nutrition Facts:
(1 serving =
1 slider, without bun)

Calories	110
Total Fiber	1g
Total Fat	3.5g
Total Carbs	5g
Total Protein	14g
Vitamin A	20%
Vitamin C	6%
Calcium	4%
Iron	6%

ULTIMATE PORTOBELLO SLIDER

4 large portobello mushrooms (or 8 small, for 2 per serving), stem removed

Cooking spray as needed

1 cup wilted baby spinach or arugula

Tomato and red onion, sliced, as needed

4 ounces aged provolone cheese slices

Romaine or iceberg lettuce as needed

Whole-wheat buns, bread, or English muffins (optional)

MARINADE

1 cup extra-virgin olive oil

1 cup aged balsamic vinegar

4 tablespoons Dijon mustard

5 cloves roasted garlic

1 tablespoon chopped roasted shallots (optional)

¼ teaspoon sea salt

¼ teaspoon freshly ground black pepper

1 cup vegetable stock

Combine all of the marinade ingredients, except for the vegetable stock, in a blender, and blend on high. Slowly pour the vegetable stock into the blender while it is still on and blend until smooth. Marinate the mushrooms for 1 hour to overnight, covered in the fridge.

Preheat grill to medium high. Grill the marinated mushrooms on both sides until soft. With the "gill" side up and the cap side down, add the wilted spinach and tomatoes, and top each with the provolone cheese. Put the sliders back onto the grill for a few minutes with the cover down to melt the cheese. Place each slider on a lettuce leaf or your bread of choice if desired, and top each with your favorite burger condiments. ✿

NUTRITION 4-1-1: MEATY MUSHROOMS

Portobello is actually a larger species of a cremini mushroom. These mushrooms have a meaty texture, which makes them ideal for grilling or as a great meat substitute.

You may want two! While portobello gives a great mouthfeel, it doesn't have a significant amount of protein; you may want to add an ounce of cheese for an additional 7 grams of protein or choose some appetizers that are protein rich.

Nutrition Facts:
(1 serving = 1 slider, without bun)

Calories	90
Total Fiber	1g
Total Fat	6g
Total Carbs	5g
Total Protein	5g
Vitamin A	10%
Vitamin C	4%
Calcium	10%
Iron	2%

7

BURGERS & SLIDERS

8 Servings • Prep: 20–25 min. • Grill: 10–15 min.

VEGETARIAN LENTIL SLIDER

1½ cups crimson lentils, cooked tender and chilled

¼ cup extra-virgin olive oil

1 red onion, finely diced

3 carrots, finely chopped

2 cloves garlic, roasted

¾ cup whole-wheat bread crumbs (more may be needed)

¼ cup roughly chopped parsley

2 large eggs or ½ cup egg substitute

½ cup plain low-fat Greek yogurt

1 teaspoon fresh lemon juice

Salt to taste

1 cup coriander seeds

¾ cup cumin seeds

1½ teaspoons turmeric

1½ teaspoons ground ginger

1½ teaspoons black peppercorns

Cooking spray as needed

Tomato and red onion, sliced, as needed

Romaine or iceberg lettuce as needed

Potato or whole-wheat buns, bread, or English muffins (optional)

Grind the coriander, cumin, turmeric, ginger, and peppercorns in a spice grinder or coffee grinder, and set aside. You will only be using 2–4 tablespoons when forming a patty. (It's always great to have extra spice mix already prepared for next time!)

Combine the chilled lentils, oil, onion, carrot, garlic, bread crumbs, parsley, and egg in a food processor, and blend until semi-smooth. Fold in the yogurt, lemon, salt, and 2–4 tablespoons of the freshly ground spices.

Preheat grill to high. Form eight slider-size patties from the lentil mixture, and place them on a piece of aluminum foil on the grill. As they cook, they will begin to "set" (but will remain fragile); at that point, flip them off of the aluminum foil to develop grill marks. Serve with your favorite burger condiments, with or without your favorite toasted bun or bread. ✿

Many people presume that if a food is vegetarian it will be lower in calories when in fact this slider is higher in carbohydrates and calories than any other slider for equal protein. There is no saturated fat, of course, and if you are vegetarian for moral or spiritual reasons, then your motivation is non-caloric anyway!

Nutrition Facts:
(1 serving =
1 slider, without bun)

Calories	330
Total Fiber	11g
Total Fat	13g
Total Carbs	43g
Total Protein	17g
Vitamin A	80%
Vitamin C	15%
Calcium	20%
Iron	70%

JERK BISON SLIDER WITH FRUIT SALSA

1 pound lean ground bison or beef

½ cup egg substitute or 2 whole eggs

½ cup puréed vegetables (note below)

¼–½ cup wet jerk seasoning (not powdered), mild, medium, or spicy

Whole-wheat bread crumbs, couscous, or instant oatmeal as needed

Salt and pepper to taste

Cooking spray as needed

Shredded romaine or iceberg lettuce as needed

Whole-wheat buns, bread, or English muffins (optional)

SALSA

½ cup small-diced papaya

½ cup small-diced mango

½ cup finely julienned red onion

½ cup small-diced green bell pepper

½ cup small-diced tomato

1 lime, juiced

¼ cup finely chopped cilantro

Salt and pepper to taste

Mix the ground bison, eggs, vegetable purée, jerk seasoning, salt, and pepper in a bowl. (The mixture may be very soft and moist at this point.) Add the binder of your choice (bread crumbs, etc.) a little at a time until the mixture becomes malleable and you can form patties. Make eight slider-sized burgers, and let them rest for 30 minutes to overnight (in the refrigerator).

Mix all of the salsa ingredients together in a bowl; season to taste; and set aside

Preheat grill to high. Lightly mist the sliders with the cooking spray to prevent sticking to the grill. Cook the slider to 145°F for medium rare or to desired doneness. Place the sliders on your choice of bread if desired; top each with the salsa; and serve with your favorite burger condiments. ✿

Note: For the vegetable purée, the kind of vegetable is not really important. The vegetables will mimic some of the properties of the missing fat, giving you a moist, tender product. When considering which vegetable to use, reflect on what is available, what flavors you like on the burgers (mushroom, onion, or wilted spinach, etc.), or what you have leftover in your refrigerator.

Fruit may not be the first thing you'd think of to pair with a burger, but give it a try. I think you will be pleasantly surprised!

Nutrition Facts:
(1 serving =
1 slider, without bun)

Calories	140
Total Fiber	1g
Total Fat	4g
Total Carbs	12g
Total Protein	14g
Vitamin A	15%
Vitamin C	45%
Calcium	4%
Iron	15%

8 Vegetables

You don't need a degree in nutrition to know that vegetables are good for you. Vegetables are high on the nutrient-rich list and low in calories; they're also high in water and fiber, which helps with filling you up without filling you out.

144 Sweet Corn with Red Pepper, Cilantro, and Lime, Chef Todd C. Gray

146 BBQ Pizza

147 Asparagus with Mustard Vinaigrette

148 Asian-Style Grill-Top Stir-Fry

149 Garden Pizza

150 Grill-Top Tomato and Parmesan

151 Braised Kale

152 Roasted-Garlic-and-Balsamic-Marinated Vegetable Kebabs

154 Portobello Pizza

155 Grilled Broccolini

156 Grilled Brussels Sprouts

157 Caraway-Flavored Baby Bok Choy

158 Mixed Mushrooms

159 Grilled-Tomato Soup

160 Eggplant Sticks with Rosemary

161 Grill-Top Baked Spinach

Cooked or Raw?

I prefer many vegetables, like broccoli, steamed or sautéed rather than raw because the small amount of cooking time helps to break down some of the fiber and, for me, makes the taste even more appealing. Adding oil can also help with absorption of some fat-soluble vitamins and phytonutrients, such as lycopene and carotinoids. Phytonutrients are a large group of components that are found in plants and have been discovered to promote health and prevent disease. They have been associated with decreasing the risk of some cancers, cardiovascular disease, and hypertension, and they may help prevent cellular damage, repair DNA, and decrease cholesterol.

The disease protection associated with phytonutrients can be found in fruits, vegetables, beans, cereals, grains, nuts, and plant-based beverages like tea and wine. Scientists have identified hundreds of phytonutrients, each with distinct health benefits, from inhibiting cancer-cell growth to stimulating the growth of beneficial bacteria in the intestinal tract. That is why we hear about "eating your colors" from the Produce for Better Health Foundation and why it is important to eat a variety of plant-based food to get all of the benefits of phytonutrients.

NUTRITION 4-1-1: LUTEIN-RICH CORN

Despite the recent bad reputation of high-fructose corn syrup, fresh corn should be part of a healthy diet because it is a good source of fiber and lutein, the compound that keeps your eyes healthy. Plus, the variety of corn used to make HFCS is not the same that you eat on the cob.

NUTRITION 4-1-1: NUTRIENT-RICH RED PEPPERS

One-half of a red bell pepper contains all the vitamin C and A a person needs in one day. This may help reduce the risk of heart attack, stroke, cataracts, blood clot formation, and elevated cholesterol levels. Red peppers have the highest nutrient value of all bell peppers.

SWEET CORN WITH RED PEPPER, CILANTRO, AND LIME

3 tablespoons extra-virgin olive oil

10–12 ears fresh corn (to yield 8 cups kernels)

1 teaspoon salt (or more to taste)

½ teaspoon freshly ground pepper

2 cups diced red pepper

1 cup thinly sliced scallion, white and green parts (2 scallions)

¼ cup julienned cilantro

2 tablespoons fresh lime juice

Preheat grill to high. Wrap the corn in aluminum foil, and cook it for about 8–12 minutes, rolling it a bit over the grill. Then cut the corn off the cob; it's so fresh and worth the effort.

Turn the grill down to medium; pour 3 tablespoons of olive oil into a large skillet; and heat it. When the oil is hot, add the corn, red pepper, salt, and pepper, and cook for 5 minutes (or less) until just cooked and no longer starchy. Remove from heat, and stir in the scallions and cilantro. Allow the salad to cool, and finish with the fresh lime juice. Serve cold or at room temperature. ✤

More than a decade ago, Chef Todd C. Gray, along with his wife and business partner, Ellen Kassoff Gray, founded Equinox Restaurant in Washington, DC. This dynamic duo has risen to the top of the city's vibrant culinary scene, developing a reputation as one of the area's most passionate and formidable hospitality and philanthropic pair. A long-time advocate for sustainable agriculture, he has worked tirelessly with local farmers to grow and use fresh organic produce and other ingredients for his kitchen. In 2011, after eight nominations, he was named the Restaurant Association of Metropolitan Washington's 2011 RAMMY Chef of the Year. He has also received five nominations for the James Beard Foundation's Best Chef, Mid-Atlantic Award. Raised in Virginia, Chef Todd studied at the University of Richmond and graduated with honors from the Culinary Institute of America.

Personal Wellness: I ride my bike to work and practice yoga. I have found that eating seasonally not only feels right but is much easier to do. I enjoy supporting local farmers and buying the food that is exactly of the moment. I believe there are 12 seasons to a year, and each year is different.

Nutrition Facts: (1 serving = ½ cup)	Calories	105	Vitamin A	7.5%
	Total Fiber	1.5g	Vitamin C	25%
	Total Fat	5.5g	Calcium	0%
	Total Carbs	14g	Iron	2%
	Total Protein	2.5g		

VEGETABLES 8

BBQ PIZZA

1 cup all-purpose or bread flour

½ cup whole-wheat flour

1 package dry yeast (about 2¼ teaspoons)

1 teaspoon salt

½–⅔ cup hot water (about 120°F)

1 tablespoon extra-virgin olive oil

1 cup sharp cheddar cheese

PIZZA SAUCE

1 cup grilled zucchini

½ cup grilled tomatoes

¼ cup roasted garlic

1 tablespoon dry oregano

1 tablespoon olive oil

1 tablespoon chili powder

Salt and pepper to taste

This pizza is a vegetable-based dish, but obviously, because of the crust, it provides starch. You can eat this as an entrée with a side salad, or you can have a small slice as a side to another entrée.

Mix all of the pizza-dough ingredients except the cheese in a stand mixer (or by hand) for 5–10 minutes. Let the dough double in size. Punch the air out of it, and reform it into a ball. Let this rest, undisturbed, for at least 15 minutes. (Depending on the kind of flour and maybe even the brand, you may need a little more or a little less water for the recipe. If you are uncomfortable making dough or don't have the time, you can buy premade whole-wheat pizza dough at most supermarkets.)

Add all of the sauce ingredients to a blender, and purée the mixture.

Preheat grill to high. Form the pizza dough, and grill it on one side just long enough to get grill marks. Flip the pizza, and add the sauce and cheese. Lower the heat to medium, and cover the grill. Cook the pizza until it's done, about 8–10 minutes. ✿

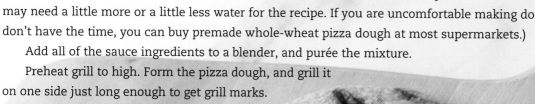

Nutrition Facts:
(1 serving = 2 ounces, or one-quarter pizza)

Calories	390
Total Fiber	5g
Total Fat	25g
Total Carbs	22g
Total Protein	17g
Vitamin A	30%
Vitamin C	15%
Calcium	45%
Iron	10%

ASPARAGUS WITH MUSTARD VINAIGRETTE

¾–1 pound asparagus, trimmed

Salt and freshly ground pepper to taste

¼ cup toasted sesame seeds

Cooking spray as needed

VINAIGRETTE

¼ cup balsamic vinegar

¼ cup extra-virgin olive oil

1 tablespoon Dijon mustard

1 clove garlic, roasted and finely chopped
   (See roasting instructions, page 153.)

1 tablespoon fresh, picked thyme

Salt and freshly ground pepper to taste

Preheat grill to medium high. Mix all of the vinaigrette ingredients in a bowl until smooth. Season the asparagus, and mist it lightly with cooking spray. Grill the asparagus to desired doneness, about 8 to 12 minutes. Serve the asparagus drizzled with the vinaigrette and topped with the sesame seeds. ✽

Of course, grilled asparagus, even without vinaigrette, is delicious (and can save some calories)!

8

VEGETABLES

NUTRITION 4-1-1: ASPARAGUS URINE

Researchers believe that, during digestion, the vegetable's sulfurous amino acids break down into smelly chemical components in all people. However, only about one-quarter of the population appears to have the special gene that allows them to smell those compounds.

Nutrition Facts:
(1 serving =
3–4 ounces asparagus)

Calories	90
Total Fiber	3g
Total Fat	6g
Total Carbs	6g
Total Protein	3g
Vitamin A	15%
Vitamin C	10%
Calcium	4%
Iron	15%

ASIAN-STYLE GRILL-TOP STIR-FRY

¼ cup low-sodium soy sauce

2 tablespoons water

1 teaspoon toasted sesame oil

    (or 1 tablespoon toasted sesame seeds)

2 tablespoons olive or canola oil

½ teaspoon red pepper flakes (optional)

2 cloves garlic, minced

2 teaspoons chopped fresh ginger root, divided

½ cup thinly sliced green onions

1 small head broccoli, florets removed & blanched

½ cup blanched snow peas

¾ cup julienned and blanched carrots

1 cup red and green bell peppers

¼ cup julienned red onion

2 cups Napa cabbage

Preheat grill to high. Preheat a perforated vegetable grilling pan or a wok. Combine the soy sauce, water, oils, pepper flakes (optional), garlic, ginger, and green onions in a large bowl. Stir to mix. Add all of the vegetables, and toss to coat them. In small batches (very important), toss the vegetables in the perforated pan or wok until the cabbage starts to wilt or to desired doneness. Remove the batch to a serving vessel, and start the next batch. (Taste to ensure proper seasoning.) Once you have cooked all of the vegetables, serve immediately. ✤

Nutrition Facts:
(1 serving = 1 cup)

Calories	120
Total Fiber	7g
Total Fat	3g
Total Carbs	19g
Total Protein	7g
Vitamin A	120%
Vitamin C	330%
Calcium	15%
Iron	10%

GARDEN PIZZA

1 cup all-purpose or bread flour

½ cup whole-wheat flour

1 package dry yeast (about 2¼ teaspoons)

1 teaspoon salt

½–⅔ cup hot water (about 120°F)

3 tablespoons extra-virgin olive oil

¼ cup minced garlic

1 cup baby spinach

½ cup seeded and diced tomatoes

½ cup julienned red onion

¼ cup ribbon cut basil

1 tablespoon dried oregano

6 ounces fresh mozzarella, chopped

Mix the flour, yeast, salt, water, and 1 tablespoon of olive oil in a stand mixer (or by hand) for 5–10 minutes. Let the dough double in size. Punch the air out of it, and reform it into a ball. Let this rest, undisturbed, for at least 15 minutes. (Depending on the kind of flour and maybe even the brand, you may need a little more or a little less water for the recipe. If you are uncomfortable making dough or don't have the time, you can buy premade whole-wheat pizza dough at most supermarkets.)

Preheat grill to high. Heat a sauté pan; add 2 tablespoons of olive oil and the garlic; and cook until the garlic starts to brown. Add the spinach, tomatoes, onion, basil, and oregano. Mix and heat for about 5 minutes.

Form the pizza dough, and grill it on one side just long enough to get grill marks. Flip the pizza, and add the cheese, topped by the vegetable mixture. Lower the heat to medium, and cover the grill. Cook the pizza until it's done, about 8–10 minutes. ✻

8

VEGETABLES

Nutrition Facts:
(1 serving = 2 ounces, or one-quarter pizza)

Calories	290
Total Fiber	2g
Total Fat	20g
Total Carbs	16g
Total Protein	9g
Vitamin A	15%
Vitamin C	10%
Calcium	4%
Iron	6%

4 Servings • Prep: 5 min. • Bake (in covered grill): 20–30 min.

GRILL-TOP TOMATO AND PARMESAN

Preheat grill to high. Arrange the tomatoes in a medium-size stovetop-and-oven-proof baking dish so that they don't touch the sides or the other tomatoes. Drizzle each tomato with oil, and top with salt and pepper. Mix the Parmesan and herbs together, and then evenly divide the cheese mixture on the tops of the tomatoes, ensuring that you don't spill too much. Bake, with the grill cover down, for 20–30 minutes or until the tomatoes become soft and the cheese crusts. Serve immediately. ✤

4 large globe tomatoes, tops cut off

2 tablespoons olive oil

Salt and pepper to taste

¼ cup finely grated Parmesan cheese

2 tablespoons chopped fresh oregano

NUTRITION 4-1-1: POTENT PARMESAN

Only a small amount of this cheese is necessary to give a recipe a salty, nutty, kick. Just one ounce (or 6 teaspoons) of Parmesan contains 11g of protein, 31% of the RDA for calcium, and 20% for phosphorus.

Nutrition Facts:
(1 serving =
one stuffed tomato)

Calories	130
Total Fiber	2g
Total Fat	10g
Total Carbs	7g
Total Protein	5g
Vitamin A	30%
Vitamin C	45%
Calcium	8%
Iron	2%

BRAISED KALE

8 cups cleaned and roughly chopped kale
    (just over 1 pound)

2 tablespoons olive oil

1 large red onion, medium diced

4 cloves garlic, minced

1½–2 cups low-sodium chicken or vegetable stock

¼ cup apple-cider vinegar

2 tablespoons freshly ground coriander

Salt and pepper to taste

Preheat grill to high. Place a large cast-iron pan on the grill to preheat. Combine the oil, onion, and garlic in the pan, and sauté until the onions become translucent. Add the kale, and stir to incorporate it. Add the stock; cover; and cook until kale becomes tender (10–15 minutes). Remove the cover, and stir in the vinegar, coriander, salt, and pepper. Serve immediately. ⌘

8

VEGETABLES

NUTRITION 4-1-1: HIGH-K KALE
Kale is a nutritional powerhouse providing 40% of the daily requirement of magnesium, 180% of vitamin A, 200% of vitamin C, and 1,020% of vitamin K per cup. And unlike most vegetables, kale thrives in colder temperatures, making it an excellent choice during the winter months.

Nutrition Facts:
(1 serving = ½ cup)

Calories	100
Total Fiber	3g
Total Fat	4.5g
Total Carbs	12g
Total Protein	4g
Vitamin A	205%
Vitamin C	135%
Calcium	10%
Iron	7.5%

These could also be served as an appetizer.

ROASTED-GARLIC-AND-BALSAMIC-MARINATED VEGETABLE KEBABS

1 cup halved white button mushrooms
   (sliced in half, lengthwise)

2 small zucchinis, cut into 1-inch cubes

1 medium red onion, cut into 1-inch cubes

½ cup whole cherry tomatoes

4–5 asparagus stalks, cut into quarters

1 fennel bulb, cut into 1-inch cubes

½ large yellow pepper, cut into 1-inch cubes

½ large orange pepper, cut into 1 inch cubes

16–32 bamboo skewers

MARINADE

1 bulb garlic, roasted
   (See roasting instructions.)

½ cup balsamic vinegar

¼ cup extra-virgin olive oil

1 sprig rosemary

½ tablespoon salt

¼ tablespoon fresh ground black pepper

8 VEGETABLES

HOW TO ROAST GARLIC

Peel away the outer layers of the garlic bulb skin, leaving the skins of the individual cloves intact. Slice the top of the cloves, exposing the individual cloves of garlic. Rub with olive oil (enough to coat each clove), wrap in aluminum foil and place in a preheated 400°F oven. Cook until aromatic and brown, about 30–35 minutes. The cloves should be soft to the touch and sweet in smell. Once the garlic has cooled, squeeze out the individual garlic cloves from the bulb. Give them a little mash, and add them to marinade.

Soak the skewers in water for about 30 minutes (to prevent them from burning and disintegrating on the grill). Combine all of the marinade ingredients into a sealable plastic bag. Thread each vegetable onto skewers in whichever order you desire. (Thread each of the veggies onto two skewers to hold better if you prefer.) Place the vegetable kebabs into the marinade bag; lay the bag flat in a large container; and put the container in the refrigerator for the kebabs to marinate for 1 hour.

Preheat grill to medium high. Mist the kebabs with a little bit of cooking spray to prevent the vegetables from sticking, and cook, turning frequently, until grill marks appear and vegetables look and feel tender. ✻

Nutrition Facts: (1 serving = two skewers, or 1 cup)	Calories	80	Vitamin A	4%
	Total Fiber	2g	Vitamin C	80%
	Total Fat	3.5g	Calcium	4%
	Total Carbs	9g	Iron	4%
	Total Protein	2g		

4 Servings • Prep: 5 min. • Grill: 15 min.

PORTOBELLO PIZZA

4 large portobello mushrooms
¾ cup tomato sauce (can be homemade or your favorite store-bought brand)
2 ounces fresh mozzarella cheese (one slice per mushroom)

Preheat grill to medium high. Clean the mushrooms with a wet paper towel; remove the stem; and clean out the "gills." Once you have prepped the mushrooms, fill them with desired amount of tomato sauce; then top each mushroom and sauce with the mozzarella. Place the mushrooms on the grill, and lower the cover. Cook until mushroom is fully done and cheese is bubbling, about 15 minutes. ⚜

Nutrition Facts: (1 serving = one portobello pizza)	
Calories	80
Total Fiber	2g
Total Fat	3.5g
Total Carbs	7g
Total Protein	5g
Vitamin A	4%
Vitamin C	8%
Calcium	0%
Iron	4%

GRILLED BROCCOLINI

Preheat grill to high. Toss the Broccolini with the oil, garlic, salt, and pepper in a bowl. Grill the Broccolini to desired doneness, about 5 to 10 minutes, and toss it in the lemon juice. Serve immediately because the acid in the lemon juice will start to turn the Broccolini brown. ✿

1 large bunch Broccolini, clean, trimmed, and blanched (about 1 pound)

2 tablespoons olive oil

2 cloves garlic, minced

Salt and pepper to taste

½ lemon, juiced

8

VEGETABLES

Nutrition Facts: (1 serving = 1 cup)	
Calories	100
Total Fiber	4g
Total Fat	7g
Total Carbs	7g
Total Protein	3g
Vitamin A	70%
Vitamin C	180%
Calcium	6%
Iron	6%

GRILLED BRUSSELS SPROUTS

1 pound Brussels sprouts, uniform in size, boiled & chilled

½ cup apple cider or rice-wine vinegar

¼ cup olive oil

1 tablespoon Dijon mustard

2 cloves garlic, minced

Salt and pepper to taste

4–6 bamboo skewers

Cooking spray as needed

Soak the skewers in water for about 30 minutes (to prevent them from burning and disintegrating on the grill).

Preheat grill to high. Combine the vinegar, oil, mustard, garlic salt, and pepper in a bowl, and stir to mix. Add the Brussels sprouts to this mixture, and toss to coat. Thread the Brussels sprouts, tip to tip, onto the skewers, making kebabs. Lightly mist the sprouts with cooking spray to prevent sticking. Grill until slightly charred on all sides, about 5–10 minutes. ⌘

Nutrition Facts:
(1 serving = 1 cup)

Calories	70
Total Fiber	4g
Total Fat	2.5g
Total Carbs	11g
Total Protein	4g
Vitamin A	15%
Vitamin C	160%
Calcium	4%
Iron	8%

CARAWAY-FLAVORED BABY BOK CHOY

4–6 baby bok choy heads, halved
1 tablespoon olive or canola oil
½ cup rice-wine vinegar
1 teaspoon crushed caraway seeds
Salt and pepper to taste
Cooking spray as needed

Mix the oil, vinegar, caraway seeds, salt, and pepper together in a bowl. Toss the bok choy halves in the mixture, and let them marinate for 10 to 30 minutes.

Preheat grill to high, and cook the bok choy until it starts to char on one side; then turn over and repeat. Remove the bok choy from the heat; adjust the seasonings; and serve.

8

VEGETABLES

Nutrition Facts:
(1 serving =
1–2 heads of bok choy)

Calories	20
Total Fiber	0g
Total Fat	1g
Total Carbs	1g
Total Protein	0g
Vitamin A	20%
Vitamin C	15%
Calcium	2%
Iron	2%

NUTRITION 4-1-1: IMPRESSIVE BOK CHOY
This tasty green vegetable has only 9 calories per cup, yet packs an impressive amount of potassium; vitamins A, C, and D; and folate.

MIXED MUSHROOMS

1 pound mixed mushrooms (wild preferred),
    clean & trimmed

¼ cup olive oil

1–2 lemons, juiced

1 red onion, medium diced

1 bunch thyme leaves, picked and rough chopped

Salt and pepper to taste

Cooking spray as needed

Mix all of the ingredients together in a bowl, and let the mushrooms marinate for 30 minutes.

Preheat grill to high. Place a perforated grilling vegetable pan on the grill top, and let it preheat as well. Carefully toss the mushroom mixture in the pan until the mushrooms begin to soften. (*Optional*: Before you remove the mushrooms from the heat, let them sit, unstirred, on high heat, to form a crust on the bottom layer of mushrooms.)

Serve immediately. ✂

Nutrition Facts:
(1 serving = ½–¾ cup)

Calories	50
Total Fiber	2g
Total Fat	2g
Total Carbs	7g
Total Protein	3g
Vitamin A	0%
Vitamin C	2%
Calcium	2%
Iron	2%

NUTRITION 4-1-1: NUTRITIOUS MUSHROOMS
Mushrooms contain around 80–90 percent water, making them low in calories, sodium, and fat. They are an excellent source of potassium (which can help lower high blood pressure and lower the risk of stroke) and rich in niacin, riboflavin, and selenium.

GRILLED-TOMATO SOUP

16 vine-ripened tomatoes,
    washed (about 4 pounds)
Salt to taste
Black pepper to taste
½ cup half and half

Preheat grill to high. Before placing the tomatoes on the grill, use a paring knife to remove the stem seat and make an X on the bottom of each. Grill the tomatoes until very soft and wrinkled.

Place the tomatoes in a large bowl, and purée to soup consistency using an emulsion blender (or regular blender). Stir in half and half, salt, and pepper. Taste the soup to make sure it is seasoned to your liking, and serve. ✻

8

VEGETABLES

Consuming soup before a meal decreases the amount of food one tends to subsequently eat.

NUTRITION 4-1-1: ANTIOXIDANT TOMATOES

Tomatoes are actually a fruit not a vegetable. They are extremely high in lycopene (a powerful antioxidant), which gives the tomato its vibrant red color. Lycopene is actually better absorbed when cooked or processed, so sauté those tomatoes, and enjoy the taste as well as the health benefits.

Grilled Polenta, page 172

Nutrition Facts:
(1 serving = 8–10 ounces)

Calories	80
Total Fiber	3g
Total Fat	4g
Total Carbs	11g
Total Protein	3g
Vitamin A	45%
Vitamin C	60%
Calcium	6%
Iron	4%

Garnish options: top with 1 tablespoon shredded cheese or some baked crispy tortilla strips.

EGGPLANT STICKS WITH ROSEMARY

1 medium eggplant, peeled

2–4 tablespoons olive oil

2 tablespoons picked and finely chopped rosemary

½ cup chopped basil

Salt and pepper to taste

1 lemon, quartered

Cut the eggplant into ½-inch "planks" on a cutting board; cut ½-inch sticks from each plank; then cut each stick to a uniform length to minimize vegetable waste. Combine the oil, herbs, salt, and pepper in a bowl, and brush the eggplant sticks with the mixture.

Preheat grill to medium high. Grill the sticks to desired doneness on one side; turn; and repeat. Remove the eggplant from the heat; squeeze the lemon quarters over the sticks; and serve immediately. ⚜

Nutrition Facts:
(1 serving =
one-quarter eggplant)

Calories	170
Total Fiber	5g
Total Fat	14g
Total Carbs	9g
Total Protein	2g
Vitamin A	6%
Vitamin C	15%
Calcium	4%
Iron	4%

NUTRITION 4-1-1: EGGPLANT SKINS

Hide your peeler (when possible)! The skin of eggplants contains the anti-cancer, antimicrobial, LDL-lowering chlorogenic acid, as well as the antioxidant nasunin, which prevents cellular damage, especially in the brain. Some recipes don't require you to peel—so don't!

GRILL-TOP BAKED SPINACH

1½–2 pounds baby spinach

2 tablespoons olive oil

½ cup finely diced white onion

Salt and pepper to taste

1 cup low-sodium chicken or vegetable stock

½ cup shredded pecorino Romano cheese (optional)

2 tablespoons toasted panko bread crumbs (optional)

Preheat grill to high. Combine the oil and onions in a medium-size stovetop-and-oven-proof casserole dish (2–4-quart size), and sauté until the onions are translucent. Add the spinach, and wilt it. (You may need to do this in batches, depending on your pan size.)

Add seasoning and the chicken or vegetable stock, and cook uncovered for 6–10 minutes. You may choose to top the casserole with cheese and bread crumbs while it cooks. Serve immediately upon removing it from the heat. ✃

8

VEGETABLES

Nutrition Facts: (1 serving = ½ cup)	
Calories	110
Total Fiber	6g
Total Fat	5g
Total Carbs	14g
Total Protein	5g
Vitamin A	80%
Vitamin C	30%
Calcium	15%
Iron	20%

9 Starches

Starch, as a category, can be confusing because, although starches are carbohydrates, they are not the only source of carbohydrates in the diet.

164 Brown-Sugar-and-White-Balsamic-Glazed Root Vegetables, Chef Maxcel Hardy

166 Grilled Sweet-Potato "Fries"

167 Orange-Glazed Acorn Squash

168 Grill-Top Baked Potato

169 Quinoa and Grilled Vegetables

170 Grill-Top Lentils

171 Grill-Top Black-Eyed Peas

172 Polenta with Creamy Mushroom Sauce

174 Wheat-Berry-and-Grilled-Vegetable Tabbouleh

175 Balsamic-Dijon Potato Salad

Starches, which are rich in carbohydrates, include
- Grain-based foods like cereal, rice, pasta, bread, quinoa, barley (and other grains).
- Starchy vegetables like peas, corn, potatoes, pumpkin, and squash.

But carbohydrates also come from fruits, beans, milk, and yogurt. In addition, all vegetables provide carbohydrates, but green vegetables are not as calorically carbohydrate-dense as starchy vegetables—providing 5 grams of carbohydrates per ½-cup portion compared with, say, 15 grams for corn. Carbohydrates also come from products that have added sugars, like soda and candy, but these are nutritionally empty carbohydrates (sometimes referred to as "carbage").

Because carbohydrates are a good source of energy, starch is often a staple in the diet: pasta, rice, and potatoes. This was traditionally an easy way for workers in the field to fill their caloric needs and sustain muscles for long days of labor. But those who work at a desk all day do not need as much fuel: 130 grams of carbohydrates is what is absolutely needed to power our brains; more is needed to fuel daily activity; and even more is needed if one regularly exercises.

There is debate within the scientific community as to exactly how much starch we need, but it seems a safe bet to say that at least three servings of whole grains a day is the way to go. A serving of whole grains equals ¼–½ cup of brown rice, quinoa, whole corn, whole wheat, barley, beans, etc. (about 15 grams of carbohydrates). These less-processed whole grains supply us with fiber, micronutrients (vitamins and minerals), and phytonutrients, all of which are beneficial to our well-being, while refined or processed grains (white rice, white bread, pretzels, cookies, etc.) do not.

So if three servings is the minimum, what if you just want more? Because a person on a weight-loss plan may be targeting 1,600 to 2,000 calories a day, that leaves anywhere from 4-9 servings from the starch group a day, depending on how much protein, fruit, vegetables, dairy, and fat you select. One cup of rice or pasta is two to three servings in just that one part of one meal. Once you add bread or rolls and dessert (clearly not whole grain, but it has to fit somewhere—or take calories away from some group), you are way over on the starch servings for a day even from one meal.

To manage weight, making choices is absolutely mandatory. Choosing to consume rolls or bread to start dinner, have a drink before the meal, and, say, order a quesadilla as an appetizer uses all of your starch portions before you choose pasta as a main dish or settle on a side that includes rice, couscous, beans, or corn—and clearly leaves no room for cookies, pie, ice cream, or candy.

Solution: watch portions; balance selections.
- Want a starch as a side? Begin with lean protein or greens.
- Want a starch as your starter? Choose greens and lean protein as your entrée.
- Want to drink and/or eat dessert? Forego starches during the meal.

Of course another option is to get fit and be more active . . . which will allow you more food/carbohydrates to work with.

WATCH THAT SUGAR!
The "discretionary allowance" of total added sugar ranges from 6 to 12 teaspoons (or 24 to 48 grams of sugar or 96 to 192 calories). Considering that one 16-ounce sweetened iced tea or lemonade provides 46 grams of sugar (184 calories), you can see that it's easy to add up those sugar calories if you're not paying attention.

164

NUTRITION 4-1-1: ROOT VEGETABLES

Root vegetables like beets and carrots absorb nutrients from the soil around them and store all of the phytonutrients in their flesh. Choose more-intensely colored vegetables for the highest levels.

Note: The sugar helps create a sweet caramelized coating, but you can experiment using less sugar, which will cut down on the carbohydrates and calories.

BROWN-SUGAR-AND-WHITE-BALSAMIC-GLAZED ROOT VEGETABLES

2 turnips, cut lengthwise

2 beets, cut into four halves

2 golden beets, cut into four halves

2 rutabagas, cut into four halves

2 sweet potatoes, cut into four pieces lengthwise

2 black radishes, cut into four halves

1 celeriac, cut into four halves

1 large leek, cut lengthwise

½ cup chopped cilantro

½ cup brown sugar

3 tablespoons white balsamic glaze

3 tablespoons olive oil

Salt and pepper to taste

Cooking spray as needed

9

STARCHES

Preheat grill to medium. Spray the grill lightly with the cooking spray. Toss the root vegetables with the olive oil, salt, and pepper in large mixing bowl, and sear them on a 45-degree angle to the grill bars. After 2–3 minutes, turn the vegetables 90 degrees, creating a diamond pattern on them. Once they are marked, flip them to the opposite side and cook to desired doneness.

While the vegetables are cooking, mix the cilantro, brown sugar, and white balsamic glaze in a mixing bowl. Remove the leek from the grill, and dice it into large pieces. Once the rest of the root vegetables are fork tender, toss them in the glaze with the diced leeks. Serve alongside your favorite grilled poultry or beef, or enjoy as entrée. ✷

As NBA All-Star Amare Stoudemire's personal chef, Maxcel Hardy works closely with The New York Knicks' nutritionists and dieticians to ensure that Stoudemire maintains the healthy diet necessary for him to perform at his best on the court. Chef Max has also established 5 Star Culinary Concepts, outsourcing chefs to other NBA players, most notably The New York Knicks' Carmelo Anthony. Some of his other past and present clients include dignitaries such as the Prince of Dubai and Academy Award-winning actor Jamie Foxx; professional athletes Brian Hall of the Boston Red Sox, NFL All Pro Santana Moss, NFL's Dwayne Bowe, former NFL All Star Warren Sapp, and former NBA star Dennis Rodman; rappers TI, Fabulous, Rick Ross, and Trina; and R&B singer Ciara, among others. In 2010 Hardy launched his humanitarian effort "One Chef Can 86 Hunger" to help combat hunger in the America. Chef Max graduated at the top of his class from Johnson & Wales University with a degree in Culinary Arts.

Personal wellness: I drink one to two full glasses of water upon waking each morning, get 20 to 30 minutes of exercise at least five days a week, eat vegetables daily at both lunch and dinner, and try to do absolutely nothing few times a week. Our lives keep getting busier and busier as we agree to more tasks and events. For our mental health, it's important to find time to do nothing, to have no responsibilities or obligations.

Nutrition Facts (1 serving = ¼ cup)				
Calories	146	Vitamin A	23%
Total Fiber	4g	Vitamin C	50%
Total Fat	4g	Calcium	5%
Total Carbs	25g	Iron	5%
Total Protein	2.5g		

GRILLED SWEET-POTATO "FRIES"

4 sweet potatoes, peeled and sliced in wedges

2–4 tablespoons olive oil

Salt and pepper to taste

1 tablespoon dark chili powder

1 lime, zested

Cooking spray as needed

A great and flavorful twist, grilled sweet potato "fries" give you a nutrient bang providing Vitamins A and C.

Boil the potato wedges for 5 minutes to soften them. Set them aside on paper towels to dry. (If your freezer has room, place the potatoes in it for 10–15 minutes for quick, efficient drying. This will, however, warm up your freezer.)

Preheat grill to medium. Toss the blanched and dried potatoes with the oil, salt, pepper, chili pepper, and lime zest. Grill the potatoes until they're marked and semi-soft, and serve immediately. ✳

Nutrition Facts:
(1 serving = ½ cup)

Calories	120
Total Fiber	3g
Total Fat	13g
Total Carbs	13g
Total Protein	1g
Vitamin A	70%
Vitamin C	20%
Calcium	2%
Iron	2%

ORANGE-GLAZED ACORN SQUASH

1 acorn squash, quartered

1 tablespoon olive or canola oil

½ cup finely diced onion

½ cup white wine (dry style preferred)

1 cup orange juice

1 tablespoon chili powder

1 tablespoon crushed juniper berries (optional)

Salt and pepper to taste

Preheat grill to high. Sauté the onions and oil in a saucepan over the grill until the onions become translucent. Add the wine, and reduce it by three-quarters. Add the orange juice, and reduce the heat to allow the mixture to simmer. When the orange juice reduces by one-quarter, add the spices and seasonings.

Reduce the grill temperature to medium. Place the squash on the grill, and baste it with the orange glaze every few minutes while rotating the squash. Cook until the squash becomes soft with a glazed crust. Serve immediately, on the rind.

I love using OJ as a marinade and flavoring agent. All natural, nutritious, and delicious.

9 STARCHES

Nutrition Facts:
(1 serving =
¼ acorn squash)

Calories	120
Total Fiber	3g
Total Fat	4g
Total Carbs	18g
Total Protein	2g
Vitamin A	25%
Vitamin C	50%
Calcium	10%
Iron	6%

4 Servings • Prep: 5 min. • Grill (bake): 1–1½ hrs.

GRILL-TOP BAKED POTATO

4 Russet Burbank potatoes, washed and dried

2–3 tablespoons olive or canola oil

2–3 teaspoons kosher salt

Freshly ground pepper to taste

2 tablespoons picked and chopped rosemary (optional)

¼ cup low-fat or fat-free sour cream (optional)

Preheat one side of grill on high, leaving the other side off or on low. Rub the potatoes with the oil, and coat them with salt (and rosemary if desired).

Wrap each potato in aluminum foil, and place them on the cooler side of the grill. Lower the lid, and bake the potatoes, using indirect heat, for 1–1½ hours or until fork tender. Serve as is or with a dollop of low fat sour cream! ✳

Nutrition Facts:
(1 serving = 1 potato, without sour cream)

Calories	130
Total Fiber	1g
Total Fat	12g
Total Carbs	6g
Total Protein	2g
Vitamin A	0%
Vitamin C	8%
Calcium	2%
Iron	8%

You can also scoop out some of the starchy middle and add some of your favorite "stuffings," like beans and cheese, fresh salsa, poached egg, or caramelized onions.

8 Servings • Prep: 10–15 min. • Grill: 5–10 min.
• Grill (cook in saucepan): 30–40 min. • Rest: 10 min.

169

QUINOA AND GRILLED VEGETABLES

2 tablespoons olive oil

½ teaspoon toasted and ground cumin seed

¼ cup minced shallots

2 cloves garlic, peeled and minced

1 cup stemmed and diced fresh shiitake mushrooms

1 zucchini, grilled and finely chopped

1 red bell pepper, grilled and finely chopped

1 teaspoon finely chopped fresh thyme leaves

1 cup washed and drained quinoa

2–2½ cups low-sodium chicken or vegetable stock

Salt and pepper to taste

Cooking spray as needed

Preheat grill to medium high. Slice the zucchini and pepper (lengthwise); mist them lightly with cooking spray to prevent sticking; and grill them 5–10 minutes, turning once, until they begin to soften. Then chop them into small pieces.

Now heat the saucepan, and when it is hot, add the oil, cumin, and shallots, cooking until translucent. Add the garlic, mushrooms, zucchini, and peppers. Lower the heat; add the thyme and quinoa; and stir to coat the grains. Add the stock; cover the saucepan; and simmer at a low temperature for 20 minutes.

Remove the saucepan from the heat, and keep it covered for 10 minutes. Fluff the quinoa with a fork when serving, and season to taste.

9

STARCHES

Naturally gluten-free, quinoa has made a comeback! High in lysine, this grain is actually a seed. It is cooked like rice and used interchangeably. It is higher in protein than most grains and provides all essential amino acids, as well as calcium, potassium, magnesium, and fiber.

Nutrition Facts:
(1 serving = ½ cup)

Calories	140
Total Fiber	6g
Total Fat	5g
Total Carbs	13.5g
Total Protein	5g
Vitamin A	15%
Vitamin C	40%
Calcium	2%
Iron	7.5%

GRILL-TOP LENTILS

1 cup dried petite French lentils

2 tablespoons extra-virgin olive oil

1 cup finely diced onion

2 tablespoons red wine

½ cup finely diced celery

1 large clove garlic, minced

1 cup grilled and rough-chopped tomatoes

1½–2 cups low-sodium beef or
    roasted vegetable stock

Salt and pepper to taste

¼ cup chopped fresh oregano

Cooking spray as needed

Preheat grill to medium. Slice one or two large tomatoes into thick slices; mist lightly with cooking spray to prevent sticking; and grill both sides until marked, about 3 minutes per side. Then chop them up roughly to make 1 cup.

Increase the heat to high, and preheat a medium saucepan. Combine the oil and onions in the saucepan, and cook until the onions are translucent. Add the red wine, celery, garlic, tomatoes, and lentils, and cook for 1 minute. Add the stock and seasoning, and simmer, uncovered, until the lentils soften. (Because of the moisture in the vegetables, you may not need all 2 cups of the stock; reserve ½ cup until you know it's needed.) Fold in the oregano, and serve. ✿

Nutrition Facts:
(1 serving = ½ cup)

Calories	140
Total Fiber	8g
Total Fat	4.5g
Total Carbs	18g
Total Protein	7g
Vitamin A	3%
Vitamin C	15%
Calcium	4%
Iron	10%

GRILL-TOP BLACK-EYED PEAS

½ pound dry black-eyed peas, rinsed and soaked overnight

2 tablespoons olive or canola oil

1 cup finely diced onion

½ cup finely diced celery

4 cloves garlic, minced

1 red bell pepper, finely diced

1 tablespoon smoked paprika

4–6 cups low-sodium chicken or vegetable stock

Salt and pepper to taste

2 tablespoons chopped fresh oregano (optional)

Preheat grill to high. Combine the oil and onions in a medium saucepan, and sauté until the onions are translucent. Add the garlic, celery, peppers, and paprika, and cook for an additional 3–5 minutes while stirring.

Drain and rinse the beans, and add them to the saucepan. Cover them with the stock, and cook for 30 minutes or until the beans become tender. Season the bean mixture with oregano (if desired), salt, and pepper, and serve. ✳

9

STARCHES

Nutrition Facts: (1 serving = ½ cup)	
Calories	105
Total Fiber	9g
Total Fat	4g
Total Carbs	12g
Total Protein	5g
Vitamin A	17.5%
Vitamin C	35%
Calcium	2%
Iron	7.5%

4 Servings • Prep: 10–15 min. • Cook: 10–20 min.
• Cool: 1-2 hrs. • Purée: 3–5 min. • Grill: 20–25 min.

POLENTA WITH CREAMY MUSHROOM SAUCE

2 tablespoons olive oil

1 tablespoon chopped shallot

½ cup white wine

½ cup whole-grain cornmeal (if possible)

½ teaspoon dried oregano

2 cups chicken or vegetable stock

¼ cup seeded and chopped tomatoes

2 tablespoons grated Parmesan cheese

½ teaspoon salt

MUSHROOM SAUCE

1 pint sliced fresh white button mushrooms

1 large shallot, quartered

1 clove garlic, peeled

1 tablespoon olive oil

¼ cup Madeira or Marsala wine

2–3 fresh sage leaves

½ cup low-fat or fat-free Greek yogurt

Salt and pepper to taste

Preheat grill to medium high, and heat up a saucepan or small pot. From the main ingredient list, add the oil and shallots, and sauté until the shallots become translucent. Add the white wine, and cook for 1–2 minutes or until the wine begins to simmer. While whisking, add the cornmeal, oregano, stock, tomatoes, cheese, and salt. Cook for an additional 3–5 minutes, and then immediately transfer the mixture to a sheet pan or baking pan, smoothing the surface, and leave it to cool for 1–2 hours. Once the polenta is fully cooled, it should be firm enough to remove from the pan and slice into single pieces. (You will most likely have more than four pieces.)

Increase the grill temperature to high to begin preparation for the sauce. Using a grill basket, coat the mushrooms, shallots, and garlic in the oil, and grill until all are soft, about 15 minutes. Transfer the cooked ingredients to a blender, and purée on high for 3–5 minutes with the wine, sage, yogurt, salt, and pepper.

Meanwhile, grill the polenta pieces at a 45° angle to the grill bars. When grill marks appear, rotate the pieces 90° to create diamond marks; then flip and repeat the process. When the polenta is done, serve it with the mushroom sauce. ✳

Nutrition Facts: (1 serving = ½ cup)	Calories	270	Vitamin A	6%
	Total Fiber	2g	Vitamin C	10%
	Total Fat	13g	Calcium	6%
	Total Carbs	22g	Iron	6%
	Total Protein	9g		

WHEAT-BERRY-AND-GRILLED-VEGETABLE TABBOULEH

1 cup wheat berries

3 cups water

¼ teaspoon salt

1 bunch parsley, finely chopped

1 bunch green onions (scallions), grilled and chopped

1 cup chopped fresh mint

2 tomatoes, grilled and chopped

1 cup grilled and chopped zucchini

¼ cup extra-virgin olive oil

¼ cup freshly squeezed lemon juice

Salt and pepper to taste

8 large leaves romaine lettuce

Cooking spray as needed

Preheat grill to high. Pour the water and salt into a saucepan; place it on the grill; and bring the water to a boil. Pour the wheat berries into the water; reduce the heat to low; and simmer them for 30–45 minutes. You will end up with more than the 1 cup of cooked wheat berries specified, but you can refrigerate the excess and keep it for about 7–10 days.

While the wheat berries are cooking, slice the tomatoes and a small zucchini into thick slices. Lightly mist the tomato and zucchini slices and the green onions with cooking spray to prevent sticking, and grill until well marked, about 5–10 minutes per side. When they are cooked, chop them into ¼-inch pieces (approximately).

When the wheat berries are cooked, combine the tomatoes, zucchini, onions, parsley, mint, oil, lemon juice, salt, and pepper. Adjust the seasonings to your taste, and serve each helping warm on a large lettuce leaf. ✿

NUTRITION 4-1-1: WHEAT BERRY

Containing the bran, germ, and endosperm, wheat berries are wheat in its most natural form. It's tough to beat this ultimate whole grain's nutritional profile.

Nutrition Facts:
(1 serving = ½ cup)

Calories	125
Total Fiber	7g
Total Fat	7.5g
Total Carbs	13g
Total Protein	3g
Vitamin A	25%
Vitamin C	30%
Calcium	5%
Iron	12.5%

BALSAMIC-DIJON POTATO SALAD

4–6 medium red bliss potatoes (about 1 pound), quartered

¼ cup chopped parsley

1 red bell pepper, julienned

½ cup finely diced red onion

3 cloves garlic, roasted and minced

½ cup balsamic vinegar

2 tablespoons Dijon mustard

Salt and pepper to taste

½ cup thinly sliced green onions (scallions)

Cooking spray as needed

Preheat grill to high. Spray the potatoes with cooking spray to prevent sticking, and season them with salt and pepper. Grill the potatoes just until marked on all sides; turn off one side of the grill; lower the cover; and use indirect heat to finish cooking them. At the same time, put the garlic cloves on aluminum foil and roast them over the heat prior to mincing. When the potatoes are fork tender, remove them from heat and rough-chop them.

Combine all of the ingredients (except for the potatoes and green onions) in a bowl, and mix them. Add the potatoes to the bowl, and coat them with the dressing you just made. Adjust the seasonings, and serve the potato salad topped with green-onion slices. ✻

9

STARCHES

Nutrition Facts:	
(1 serving = ½ cup)	
Calories	150
Total Fiber	4g
Total Fat	0g
Total Carbs	32g
Total Protein	4g
Vitamin A	15%
Vitamin C	70%
Calcium	4%
Iron	10%

10 Desserts

Some people are dessert eaters; others, not so much. There's no reason to eat dessert. Clearly, all of the nutrients we need can be consumed from the meals and healthy snacks we eat. Yet …

178 Grilled Bananas, Chef Elizabeth Karmel

180 Grilled Strawberries with Balsamic Port Glaze, Blue Cheese, and Walnuts, Chef Elizabeth Karmel

182 Grilled Figs with Orange Balsamic Glaze, Mascarpone, and Slivered Almonds

183 Grilled-Peach Melba

184 Grilled Apple Cobbler

185 Grilled Angel Food Cake S'mores

186 Grilled Pineapple

187 Grilled-Fruit Parfait

Be "Dessert-Sensible"

We all give in to dessert once in a while. Dessert tends to feel indulgent, perhaps decadent, and for some, a perverse thought warp goes something like "I've had a hard day; I deserve dessert." This type of thinking is not so helpful or healthy. You deserve to be at a weight that is healthy and productive for your life and goals. Dessert can often sabotage that goal.

One serving of Chocolate Molten Cake from Chili's is 1,090 calories, more than half the calories many of you need in one day, never mind at the end of a complete meal! One slice of White Chocolate Raspberry Cheesecake at Olive Garden is 890 calories, and Applebee's Sizzling Apple Pie is 910 calories. Each of these examples has more calories that one complete *Grill Yourself Skinny* meal, which includes an appetizer, entrée, and 2 side dishes that nourish and fuel your body and mind.

If you are someone who has a hankering for something sweet after you eat, then for sure, try to at least share a dessert. Focus on the taste, texture, and sensation of what you are eating, and savor each bite to make it count. Try lower-calorie alternatives like sweet berries with a chocolate drizzle on top or some grilled fruit.

Balance your choices. If you know you are going to eat dessert, skip the alcohol or sweet drink, extra bread, or heavy appetizer, and save some calories for dessert. A general rule of thumb is that 10–15 percent of our daily calories can come from "discretionary," or non-nutritive, calories. This allows for approximately 200 calories for someone on a 2,000-calorie regimen. In the pages that follow, you will find some wonderfully sweet-tooth-satisfying options, most fewer than 200 calories.

A very sweet way to conclude *Grill Yourself Skinny!* Enjoy…

DESSERTS
Use your carbohydrates and calories wisely and carefully! Dessert may be worth it to you—just be sure to count them, not just skip over them as you might a word that you do not know in a novel.

GRILLED BANANAS

4 bananas (not too ripe), unpeeled

2 tablespoons sugar

2 teaspoons ground cinnamon

Pinch of fine-grain sea salt

Cooking spray, as needed

Slice the bananas, in their skins, in half lengthwise. Set them aside on a clean platter. In a small bowl, combine the sugar, cinnamon, and salt. Sprinkle the cinnamon-sugar on the cut sides of the bananas. Let the bananas sit for 5 minutes.

Preheat grill to medium low, and mist the grates with cooking spray to prevent sticking. Place the bananas, cut-side down, on the center of a clean cooking grate, and cover. Grill for 2 minutes or until grill marks appear. Using a pair of long-handled tongs, turn the banana pieces over, and cook 5 more minutes or until the skin pulls away from the bananas.

Remove the bananas from the grill, and serve them immediately. Serve them on their own, with your favorite accompaniment, or by the variations at the bottom of page 179.

North Carolina native Elizabeth Karmel, a.k.a. Grill Girl (girlsatthegrill.com), and often referred to as Queen of the Grill, is a nationally respected authority on grilling, barbecue, and Southern food. She is the Executive Chef of Hill Country Barbecue Market in New York, NY, and Washington, DC, as well as New York's Hill Country Chicken. She developed the award-winning concept, menu, and flavor profiles for all three restaurants. As a sought-after media personality, Chef Elizabeth writes for and is frequently featured in an array of national magazines, from *Saveur* to *Better Homes & Gardens*, and appears regularly on all three network morning shows. She writes a bi-monthly column for the Associated Press called "The American Table." She is also the author of three acclaimed cookbooks.

Personal Wellness: I love to learn and experience new things outside of my daily life. Last summer I took a two-week hot-glass-blowing class at The Penland School of Crafts. I fell in love with it! It was 100°F outside and 1,800°F degrees inside the glass furnace. Just goes to show you that I am drawn to fire, whether I am cooking on it or blowing glass!

Says Elizabeth Karmel: I first grilled bananas at a barbecue contest when, looking for something to eat besides pork, I spied my forgotten breakfast banana. I was living in New Orleans and had a love-hate relationship with the butter-and-sugar-soaked sautéed Bananas Foster. I loved the flavor but hated the mess and the absurd amounts of sugar and butter—calories—that are associated with the classic preparation. Well, hallelujah! Grilled bananas to the rescue. Exploding with flavor, these cinnamon-spiced bananas taste every bit as good as the original, with all of the sweetness coming from the fruit itself—slimmed down by the grill.

DIY Grilled Banana Split: Serve grilled bananas with a variety of frozen yogurt, sorbet, low-fat ice cream, or homemade ganache and caramel sauce, nuts, and toppings. Let everyone customize his or her own sundae.

"N'awlins" Variation: Serve the grilled bananas on top of vanilla ice cream, and drizzle with bourbon and toasted pecans before serving.

Nutrition Facts				
(1 serving = ½ banana)	Calories	60	Vitamin A	0%
	Total Fiber	2g	Vitamin C	8%
	Total Fat	0g	Calcium	0%
	Total Carbs	16g	Iron	2%
	Total Protein	1g		

**NUTRITION 4-1-1:
DAILY DAIRY**
Studies show that three
servings of milk, cheese, or
yogurt per day may help you
maintain a healthy weight.

GRILLED STRAWBERRIES WITH BALSAMIC PORT GLAZE, BLUE CHEESE, AND WALNUTS

1 cup good-quality port wine

1 cup balsamic vinegar

12 extra-large long-stemmed strawberries

1 tablespoon untoasted walnut oil

3 ounces favorite blue cheese, at room temperature

12–18 toasted walnut halves

Preheat grill to high. Combine the vinegar and port in a small saucepan; bring the mixture to a boil; and continue cooking until it's reduced by one-half, about 20–30 minutes. The mixture should have the consistency of a glaze thick enough to coat the back of a spoon. Reduce the heat to low, and keep the mixture warm.

Meanwhile, brush the strawberries lightly on all sides with the walnut oil. Place the fruit in the center of a very clean cooking grate, and grill over low heat until just beginning to brown, 1½ to 2 minutes. Turn the fruit over, and grill 1 minute.

Remove the strawberries from the grill, and place two strawberries on each dessert plate. Drizzle them with the glaze. Slice the cheese into six equal pieces, and arrange on the plates along with two or three toasted walnut halves. ✕

Another recipe from Chef Elizabeth Karmel

Fruit, cheese, and walnuts team up to make an easy but elegant summer dessert. Large long-stemmed strawberries are grilled quickly to warm the natural sugars and intensify their flavor. The berries are glazed with a rich port-and-balsamic-vinegar reduction and served with blue cheese and crunchy walnuts for a richly satisfying dessert that is both sophisticated and simple.

Nutrition Facts (1 serving = 2 strawberries, ½ ounce cheese)			
Calories	220	Vitamin A	2%
Total Fiber	1g	Vitamin C	50%
Total Fat	10g	Calcium	10%
Total Carbs	18g	Iron	4%
Total Protein	4g		

GRILLED FIGS WITH ORANGE BALSAMIC GLAZE, MASCARPONE, AND SLIVERED ALMONDS

8 mission figs, sliced in half

2 tablespoons toasted slivered almonds

2 tablespoons mascarpone

¼ teaspoon orange zest

8 thin strips orange peel

ORANGE BALSAMIC GLAZE

¼ cup balsamic vinegar (will reduce when cooked)

½ cup fresh orange juice

½ teaspoon orange zest

1 tablespoon clover, orange blossom, or agave honey

Preheat grill to medium high. Grill the figs for 10 minutes, turning once.

Combine the glaze ingredients in a pot, and heat the mixture on the grill. Cook the glaze until it reduces by one-half and becomes a honey consistency, about 20–30 minutes.

Mix the orange zest into the mascarpone in a small bowl.

Take the figs off the grill. Assemble them on a plate; drizzle them with a small amount of glaze; and place a small dollop of the mascarpone mixture in the center of each. Garnish the figs with the almonds and the thin strips of orange peel.

Nutrition Facts:
(1 serving = two figs)

Calories	200
Total Fiber	3g
Total Fat	9g
Total Carbs	26g
Total Protein	3g
Vitamin A	8%
Vitamin C	30%
Calcium	8%
Iron	4%

NUTRITION 4-1-1: FANTASTIC FIGS

There's more to figs than Nabisco's Newton cookies, especially for those looking for a non-dairy source of calcium: 100 grams of the fruit (equivalent to a small apple) contains 250 mg of calcium.

4 servings • Prep: 5–10 min. • Simmer (syrup): 15–20 min. • Simmer (peaches): 5–10 min. • Grill: 5 min.

183

GRILLED-PEACH MELBA

2 ripe peaches, peeled, pitted, and cut in quarters

½ cup sugar

1 cup water

1 slice fresh ginger

1 lemon, juiced

1 vanilla bean, split in half and scraped

1 cup thawed frozen raspberries

2 scoops frozen vanilla yogurt

NUTRITION 4-1-1: PEACH BENEFITS

A study in China showed that consuming fruits high in fiber, vitamin C, and carotene, such as peaches, twice per week is strongly associated with low oral cancer risk.

10

DESSERTS

The morning of or the day before you plan on serving this dessert, simmer the sugar, water, ginger slice, lemon, and vanilla bean in a saucepan until well incorporated and slightly thickened and syrupy.

Simmer the peaches in this syrup for 5–10 minutes or until they start to soften. Remove them from the heat, and let them cool. Strain the syrup, and reserve it for the raspberry sauce. Blend the raspberries in a blender, sweetening the sauce with the reserved syrup. (You may need to strain this sauce if the raspberry seeds don't blend well.)

Preheat grill to high. Grill the peach quarters just until they are marked to warm them back up. Serve immediately, dressed with the raspberry sauce and ½ scoop of vanilla frozen yogurt.

Nutrition Facts: (1 serving = ½ peach, ½ scoop of frozen yogurt)	
Calories	170
Total Fiber	2g
Total Fat	0g
Total Carbs	43g
Total Protein	3g
Vitamin A	4%
Vitamin C	35%
Calcium	6%
Iron	2%

6 servings • Prep: 10–15 min. • Simmer: 25–30 min. • Chill: 1–2 hrs.
• Grill: 6–10 min. • Bake: 20–30 min.

GRILLED APPLE COBBLER

4 Granny Smith apples, quartered, core removed

¼ sugar

½ cup water

½ lemon, juiced

1 tablespoon softened butter

¼ cup packed dark brown sugar

1 pinch salt

2 tablespoons maple syrup

1 tablespoon lime juice

1 teaspoon vanilla extract

1 large egg

¾ cup all-purpose flour

¼ cup toasted and chopped walnuts (optional)

¼ cup dried cranberries or raisins (optional)

Simmer the sugar, water, and lemon juice in a saucepan. When it becomes slightly syrupy, add the apples, and simmer them for 5–10 minutes or until they start to soften. Remove the apples from the syrup, and chill them for an hour or two.

Preheat grill to high. Grill the cooled apples until they are marked on both cut sides, about 3–5 minutes per side. Dice the apple quarters into medium-size pieces, and place them in an ovenproof glass or ceramic pie plate.

Place the rest of the ingredients, except for the flour, in a small food processor. (If you don't have a small food processor, you will want to do this by hand because a large food processor will just spread and not mix the ingredients.) Add the flour, and pulse until incorporated—do not overmix! The mixture should look like wet cookie dough.

Using a teaspoon, drop lumps of this mixture over your apples, and bake until crisp (20–30 minutes). If you'd like, add the walnuts and cranberries or raisins to the pie pan, with the apples, before covering with the cobbler mixture.

Nutrition Facts: (1 serving = ½ cup without walnuts and cranberries)

Calories	200
Total Fiber	4g
Total Fat	2.5g
Total Carbs	38g
Total Protein	3g
Vitamin A	4%
Vitamin C	10%
Calcium	2%
Iron	6%

Nutrition Facts: (1 serving = ½ cup with walnuts and cranberries)

Calories	250
Total Fiber	5g
Total Fat	6g
Total Carbs	44g
Total Protein	3g
Vitamin A	4%
Vitamin C	10%
Calcium	2%
Iron	8%

GRILLED ANGEL FOOD CAKE S'MORES

8 ½-inch-thick slices angel food cake

4 1-ounce chocolate bars,
    preferably 35% or more cocoa

8 large marshmallows (about 3 ounces)

4 pinches salt

Preheat grill to medium. Make four s'more sandwiches consisting of two slices of angel food cake, a piece of chocolate and two marshmallows, sprinkled with a small pinch of salt. Wrap each sandwich in aluminum foil, and place on the grill, on an upper rack, or cook the sandwich using indirect heat. In 5 minutes, check one to make sure it is starting to melt.

Remove the sandwiches from the foil, and grill quickly on each side to mark them. Place the sandwiches diagonally to the grates until marked; turn 90°; and mark again to create diamond shapes. Serve the sandwiches, sliced in half, with a glass of milk. ✖

10

DESSERTS

Nutrition Facts:
(1 serving = ½ sandwich)

Calories	160
Total Fiber	1g
Total Fat	2.5g
Total Carbs	30g
Total Protein	3g
Vitamin A	0%
Vitamin C	0%
Calcium	4%
Iron	0%

4 servings • Prep: 5 min. • Grill: 6–10 min.

GRILLED PINEAPPLE

1 ripe pineapple, peeled
    and quartered lengthwise

2 tablespoons clover honey

¼ cup dark rum

1 teaspoon canola oil

1 tablespoon fresh lime juice

½ teaspoon ground cinnamon

Preheat grill to high. Combine the honey, rum, oil, lime juice, and cinnamon in a bowl, and pour this mixture over the pineapple quarters. Grill the pineapple until it's marked on all sides. Remove it from the heat, and let it cool.

When the pineapple is cool enough to handle, dice it into ¼- to ½-inch chunks. To assemble for serving, place the chunks of pineapple in hollowed-out pineapple rinds for family style or in small bowls for individual servings. ✄

Nutrition Facts:
(1 serving = ¾–1 cup)

Calories	190
Total Fiber	3g
Total Fat	1.5g
Total Carbs	39g
Total Protein	1g
Vitamin A	2%
Vitamin C	180%
Calcium	4%
Iron	4%

GRILLED-FRUIT PARFAIT

4 low-fat oatmeal cookies

2 cups low-fat or fat-free Greek yogurt, vanilla flavored

2 tablespoons maple syrup (optional)

1 banana, sliced lengthwise

2 nectarines, halved

1 cup sliced strawberries (about 1/8 inch thick)

1 tablespoon sugar (optional)

4 fresh spearmint sprigs

Preheat grill to medium. Grill the fruit on each side until marked, about 3–5 minutes. Remove the fruit from the grill, and dice the banana and nectarine halves into uniform medium-size pieces. Leave the strawberries as slices. (If the fruit pieces are not sweet enough on their own, sprinkle them with sugar). If the yogurt isn't sweet enough, add a little maple syrup to sweeten it. In a stemmed drinking glass that is taller than it is wide, add a little yogurt, being extra careful not to drip any down the side of the glass. Then add a little of the fruit, again making sure not to dirty the side of the glass. Then add one-half oatmeal cookie, crumbled. Repeat this procedure until you reach the top of the glass (make sure you portion enough for 4 servings if you are using a large glass). Garnish with a sprig of mint. ✥

Note: Be sure to keep your grilled fruit separate until the last minute, to ensure the juices don't bleed into one another. Also, any healthy pastry can substitute for the cookie. Whole-grain muffins, cake, or granola bars are just some suggestions.

Nutrition Facts:
(1 serving =
1 parfait or 1 glass)

Calories	220
Total Fiber	4g
Total Fat	2.5g
Total Carbs	41g
Total Protein	12g
Vitamin A	6%
Vitamin C	10%
Calcium	10%
Iron	4%

INDEX

A

Acorn squash, Orange-Glazed, 167
Ahmad, Christopher S., 71
Alcoholic drinks, 12
Angel Food Cake, Grilled, S'Mores, 185
Antioxidants, 80, 90, 110, 159
Antipasto, Garden Veggie, 62–63
Appetizers, 34–51
    Bruschetta with Apples and Goat Cheese, 48
    chain-restaurant, 35
    Chicken Satay with Fiery Grilled-Mango Dipping
        Sauce, 38
    Grilled-and-Stuffed Potato Skins, 51
    Grilled-Beet Carpaccio, 40
    Grilled Crab Cakes, 42
    Grilled Edamame with Soy-Miso Glaze, 39
    Grilled Mushroom Lettuce Wraps, 44–45
    Guacamole-Style Edamame, 41
    Korean-Style Chicken Lettuce Wraps, 46
    Lettuce Wraps of Grilled Tofu and Moroccan
        Couscous with Spicy Tomato Chutney, 50
    Pepper-and-Garlic Hummus, 47
    Santa Barbara Prawns with Organic Tequila and
        Lime Kefir Sauce, 36–37
    Spinach-Stuffed Artichoke Hearts, 49
    Watermelon-and-Feta Skewers, 43
Apples
    Grilled Apple Cobbler, 184
    Grilled Apple Stuffed with Oatmeal, 22
    Grilled Chicken Salad on Toast, 98
    Turkey Drumstick with Apple-Maple BBQ Sauce,
        92
    Whole-Wheat Bruschetta with Apples and Goat
        Cheese, 48
Apricots
    Lettuce Wraps of Grilled Tofu and Moroccan
        Couscous with Spicy Tomato Chutney, 50
Arctic Char with Pepper Guacamole, 72
Artichokes
    Artichoke-Miso-Sauce-Marinated Cod, 83
    Cervena Venison Medallions with Pancetta,
        Toasted-Fennel-Seed Crust, Grilled Summer
        Vegetables, and Walnut Pesto, 112–113
    Mediterranean Whole Fish with Tomato-
        Artichoke Bruschetta, 80–81
    Spinach-Stuffed Artichoke Hearts, 49
Arugula
    Arugula-and-Roquefort-Stuffed Pork Chops, 124
    Grilled-Beet Carpaccio, 40
Asian-Style Grill-Top Stir-Fry, 148
Asparagus
    Asparagus with Mustard Vinaigrette, 147
    Cervena Venison Medallions with Pancetta,
        Toasted-Fennel-Seed Crust, Grilled Summer
        Vegetables, and Walnut Pesto, 112–113
    Garden Veggie Antipasto, 62–63
    Grilled Steak and Eggs, 27
    Warm Flank Steak, Tomato, and Asparagus Salad,
        58
Asparagus urine, 147
Avocado, 72
    Grilled Arctic Char with Pepper Guacamole, 41
    Grilled Pork with Avocado Salsa, 122

B

Balsamic-Dijon Potato Salad, 175
Bamboo skewers
    Cervena Venison Medallions with Pancetta,
        Toasted-Fennel-Seed Crust, Grilled Summer
        Vegetables, and Walnut Pesto, 112–113
    Chicken Satay with Fiery Grilled-Mango Dipping
        Sauce, 38
    Grilled Brussels Sprouts, 156
    Roasted-Garlic-and-Balsamic Marinated
        Vegetable Kebabs, 153
    Sugar-Cane-Skewered, Tequila-Lime-Marinated
        Shrimp, 73
    Turkey-and-Coconut Meatballs with Spicy Peanut
        Sauce, 93
    Watermelon-and-Feta Skewers, 43
Bananas
    Grilled Apple Stuffed with Oatmeal, 22
    Grilled Bananas, 178–179
    Grilled Fruit over Yogurt, 26
    Grilled Fruit Parfait, 187
    Grilled Peanut-Butter-and-Banana Sandwiches,
        28
    Skirt Steak with Pepper Chimichurri Sauce, 120
Basil

Grilled-Beet Salad with Balsamic Pesto, 57
    Tomato, Chickpea, and Onion Salad with Grilled-
        Lemon Vinaigrette, 56
Basilone, Angelo, 91
BBQ, 5
    Asian-Style BBQ Pork Tenderloin, 121
    BBQ Pizza, 146
    Honey-Mustard BBQ Turkey, 94
    Turkey Drumstick with Apple-Maple BBQ Sauce,
        92
Beef
    Coffee-Mole-Rubbed Filet Mignon, 115
    Filet Mignon with Red-Grape Sauce, 118
    Flatiron Steak with Creamy Horseradish Sauce,
        119
    grass-fed versus corn-fed, 110
    Grilled Steak and Eggs, 27
    Jerk Bison Slider with Fruit Salsa, 141
    Sirloin Carnitas with Chili-Lime Sour Cream, 117
    Skirt Steak with Pepper Chimichurri Sauce, 120
    Warm Flank Steak, Tomato, and Asparagus Salad,
        58
Beets, 164
    Brown-Sugar-and-White-Balsamic-Glazed Root
        Vegetables, 165
    Grilled-Beet Carpaccio, 40
    Grilled-Beet Salad with Balsamic Pesto, 57
    Pickled Beets, 136
    Santa Barbara Prawns with Organic Tequila and
        Lime Kefir Sauce, 36–37
Belgium endive
    Bruschetta with Apples and Goat Cheese, 48
Bell peppers. See also Green bell peppers; Orange bell
    peppers; Red bell peppers; Yellow bell peppers
    Arctic Char with Pepper Guacamole, 41
    Pepper Chimichurri Sauce, 120
Beverages, weight loss and, 12–13
Bibb lettuce
    Grilled Mushroom Lettuce Wraps, 44–45
    Korean-Style Chicken Lettuce Wraps, 46
    Lettuce Wraps of Grilled Tofu and Moroccan
        Couscous with Spicy Tomato Chutney, 50
    Philippine-Inspired Pork Lettuce Wraps, 123
Bison, 111
    Bison Sirloin Tip with Garlic-Balsamic Beet Sauce,
        127
    Jerk Bison Slider with Fruit Salsa, 141
Black beans, 90
    Chipotle Turkey Tenderloin with Roasted-Corn-
        and-Black-Bean Salsa, 91
Blackened Salmon with Grilled Maple Butternut
    Squash, 86
Blackened Seasoning, 86
Black-eyed Peas, Grill-Top, 171
Bok choy, 157
    Caraway-Flavored Baby Bok Choy, 157
    Teriyaki Chicken Slider, 132
Braised Kale, 151
Breads, whole-wheat
    Chicken Souvlaki with Cucumber Sauce on
        Whole-Wheat Pita, 102
    Grilled Peanut-Butter-and-Banana Sandwiches,
        28
Breakfast, 18–33
    benefits of eating, 18
    characteristics of good, 19
    eggs in, 19, 24
    Grilled Apple Stuffed with Oatmeal, 22
    Grilled Breakfast Pizza, 32–33
    Grilled Fruit over Yogurt, 26
    Grilled Peanut-Butter-and-Banana Sandwiches,
        28
    Grilled Salmon "Eggs Benedict" over Sweet Potato
        Latkes, 24–25
    Grilled Steak and Eggs, 27
    Grilled Turkey Chorizo Chilaquiles, 20–21
    Grill-Top Baked Eggs with Salsa, 29
    Grill-Top Vegetable Frittata, 23
    reasons for eating, 19
    Scrambled Tofu with Potato, Lentil, and Sweet
        Onion Hash, 30–31
Brick Chicken, 97
Brines, 9
Broccoli
    Asian-Style Grill-Top Stir-Fry, 148
    Grilled Breakfast Pizza, 32–33
Broccolini, Grilled, 155
Brown, Graham, 112
Brown rice
    Philippine-Inspired Pork Lettuce Wraps, 123
Brown-Sugar-and-White-Balsamic-Glazed Root
    Vegetables, 165
Bruschetta
    Bruschetta with Apples and Goat Cheese, 48
    Mediterranean Whole Fish with Tomato-

Artichoke Bruschetta, 80–81
Brussels sprouts, Grilled, 156
Burgers and sliders, 128–141
    Cervena Venison Sliders with Three Toppings,
        136–137
    Jerk Bison Slider with Fruit Salsa, 141
    Lean Ground Pork with Asian Slaw, 135
    Mustard-and-Mint Ground Lamb with Feta-
        Yogurt Sauce, 134
    Salmon Slider, 138
    Teriyaki Chicken Slider, 132
    Tuna Slider with Wasabi Spread, 131
    Turkey-Cranberry Slider with Green Bean Pesto,
        133
    Ultimate Portobello Slider, 139
    Vegetarian Lentil Slider, 140
Butternut squash
    Blackened Salmon with Grilled Maple Butternut
        Squash, 86
    Wild-Rice-Stuffed Chicken Breast with Maple-
        Butternut-Squash Sauce, 95

C

Cabbage, 135. See also Napa cabbage
    Korean-Style Chicken Lettuce Wraps, 46
    Lean Ground Pork with Asian Slaw, 135
    Ostrich with Jicama Slaw, 109
Caesar Dressing, 61
Cannellini beans
    Cedar-Plank-Grilled Salmon Fillets with Mustard-
        Dill-and-Cannellini-Bean Sauce, 77
Caraway-Flavored Baby Bok Choy, 157
Carbohydrates, 163
Carotinoids, 143
Carrots, 164
    Asian-Style Grill-Top Stir-Fry, 148
    Ostrich with Jicama Slaw, 109
Cayenne, 10
Cedar planks
    Cedar-Plank-Grilled Salmon Fillets with Mustard-
        Dill-and-Cannellini-Bean Sauce, 77
    Grilled Clams with Spinach and Celery, 87
Celeriac
    Brown-Sugar-and-White-Balsamic-Glazed Root
        Vegetables, 165
Celery, Grilled Clams with Spinach and, 87
Cervena venison, 111
    Balsamic-Glazed Cervena Kebabs with Sweet
        Peppers, Cipollini Onions, and Fennel Slaw, 116
    Cervena Venison Medallions with Pancetta,
        Toasted-Fennel-Seed Crust, Grilled Summer
        Vegetables, and Walnut Pesto, 112–113
    Cervena Venison Sliders with Three Toppings,
        136–137
    Grilled Cervena Venison Chops, 114
Ceviche, Vegetable-and-Scallop, 84
Cherries
    Duck with Cherry-Port-Wine Sauce, 105
Cherry tomatoes
    Grilled Corn and Tomato Salad, 67
    Roasted-Garlic-and-Balsamic-Marinated
        Vegetable Kebabs, 152–153
    Sugar-Cane-Skewered, Tequila-Lime-Marinated
        Shrimp, 73
    Wild-Rice-Stuffed Chicken Breast with Maple-
        Butternut-Squash Sauce, 95
Chicken, 89
    Brick Chicken, 97
    Chicken Fajita, 100–101
    Chicken Meatball Kebobs with Mango-Papaya
        Sauce, 103
    Chicken Satay with Fiery Grilled-Mango Dipping
        Sauce, 38
    Chicken Souvlaki with Cucumber Sauce on
        Whole-Wheat Pita, 102
    Grilled Chicken Salad, 98
    Korean-Style Chicken Lettuce Wraps, 46
    Shredded Chicken with Grilled Corn Cakes, 99
    Tandoori Spice-Rubbed Chicken, 96
    Teriyaki Chicken Slider, 132
    Wild-Rice-Stuffed Chicken Breast with Maple-
        Butternut-Squash Sauce, 95
Chick peas
    Tomato, Chickpea, and Onion Salad with Grilled-
        Lemon Vinaigrette, 56
Chilaquiles, 21
Chili-Lime Sour Cream, 117
Chili-Rubbed Tuna with Pepper Yogurt Sauce, 76
Chipotle peppers
    Chipotle Turkey Tenderloin with Roasted-Corn-
        and-Black-Bean Salsa, 91
Chipotle Sour Cream, 99
Chipotle Turkey Tenderloin with Roasted-Corn-and-

Black-Bean Salsa, 91
Chive-Pesto-Marinated Salmon Steaks, 82
Chocolate
　Grilled Angel Food Cake S'Mores, 185
Choline, 19
Chutney, Spicy Tomato, 50
Cilantro, 120
　Grilled Scallops with Green Curry Lentils, 85
　Sweet Corn with Red Pepper, Cilantro, and Lime,
　　145
Cinnamon, 10
Cipollini onions
　Balsamic-Glazed Cervena Kebabs with Sweet
　　Peppers, Cipollini Onions, and Fennel Slaw, 116
Clams
　Grilled Clams with Spinach and Celery, 87
　Grilled Seafood Paella, 74
Clementines
　Fennel, Clementine, and Grilled Ricotta Salata
　　Salad, 60
Coconut
　Turkey-and-Coconut Meatballs with Spicy Peanut
　　Sauce, 93
Cod
　Artichoke-Miso-Sauce-Marinated Cod, 83
　Grilled Seafood Paella, 74
Coffee, 115
Confetti, making, 37
Corn
　Chipotle Turkey Tenderloin with Roasted-Corn-
　　and-Black-Bean Salsa, 91
　Grilled Corn and Tomato Salad, 67
　as source of lutein, 144
　Sweet Corn with Red Pepper, Cilantro, and Lime,
　　145
Corn Cakes, 99
Cottage cheese
　Spinach-Stuffed Artichoke Hearts, 49
Couscous
　Grilled Crab Cakes, 42
　Lettuce Wraps of Grilled Tofu and Moroccan
　　Couscous with Spicy Tomato Chutney, 50
Crab, Grilled Cakes, 42
Cranberries
　Turkey-Cranberry Slider with Green Bean Pesto,
　　133
Creamy Horseradish Sauce, 119
Cucumber
　Chicken Souvlaki with Cucumber Sauce on
　　Whole-Wheat Pita, 102
　Grilled Sardines over Greek Salad, 59
　Santa Barbara Prawns with Organic Tequila and
　　Lime Kefir Sauce, 36–37
　Sea Bass with Tropical Salsa, 78
Curry, Green, 85

D
Dairy, 180
Desserts, 176–187
　from chain restaurants, 177
　Grilled Angel Food Cake S'Mores, 185
　Grilled Apple Cobbler, 184
　Grilled Bananas, 178–179
　Grilled Figs with Orange Balsamic Glaze,
　　Mascarpone, and Slivered Almonds, 182
　Grilled-Fruit Parfait, 187
　Grilled-Peach Melba, 183
　Grilled Pineapple, 186
　Grilled Strawberries with Balsamic Port Glaze,
　　Blue Cheese, and Walnuts, 181
Dry rubs, 9
Duck, 89
　Duck with Cherry-Port-Wine Sauce, 105
　Duck with Plum Sauce, 106
　Tea-Spice Duck Breast, 104

E
Edamame, 39
　Grilled Edamame with Soy-Miso Glaze, 39
　Guacamole-Style Edamame, 41
Eggplant
　Eggplant Sticks with Rosemary, 160
　Garden Veggie Antipasto, 62–63
　skin of, 160
Eggs
　Grilled Breakfast Pizza, 32–33
　Grilled Salmon "Eggs Benedict" over Sweet Potato
　　Latkes, 24–25
　Grilled Steak and Eggs, 27
　Grill-Top Baked Eggs with Salsa, 29
　Grill-Top Vegetable Frittata, 23

F
Fajita
　Chicken breasts, 100–101
Farmerie, Brad, 54
Fennel, 54
　Cervena Venison Medallions with Pancetta,
　　Toasted-Fennel-Seed Crust, Grilled Summer
　　Vegetables, and Walnut Pesto, 112–113
　Fennel, Clementine, and Grilled Ricotta Salata
　　Salad, 60
　Fennel Slaw, 116
　Garden Veggie Antipasto, 62–63
　Moroccan Grilled-Fennel Salad, 55
Feta cheese
　Feta-Yogurt Sauce, 134
　Watermelon-and-Feta Skewers, 43
Fiery Mango Dipping Sauce, 38
Figs, Grilled, with Orange Balsamic Glaze, Mascarpone,
　and Slivered Almonds, 182
Filet mignon
　Coffee-Mole-Rubbed Filet Mignon, 115
　Filet Mignon with Red-Grape Sauce, 118
Fish. See also Seafood
　wild caught versus farm raised, 83
Food safety, 7–8
Frittata, Grill-Top Vegetable, 23
Fruits. See also specific by name
　Grilled Fruit over Yogurt, 26
Fruit Salsa, 141

G
Garbanzo beans
　Pepper-and-Garlic Hummus, 47
Garden Pizza, 149
Garden Veggie Antipasto, 62–63
Garlic, 10
Ginger Grilled Lobster, 70–71
Glazes, Orange Balsamic, 182
Glucosinolates, 119
Goat cheese
　Bruschetta with Apples and Goat Cheese, 48
　lactose-free, 48
　Tossed Mushrooms and Baby Spinach, 65
Grape tomatoes
　Lettuce Wraps of Grilled Tofu and Moroccan
　　Couscous with Spicy Tomato Chutney, 50
　Warm Flank Steak, Tomato, and Asparagus Salad,
　　58
Gray, Todd C., 145
Greek yogurt
　Chicken Souvlaki with Cucumber Sauce on
　　Whole-Wheat Pita, 102
　Chili-Rubbed Tuna with Pepper Yogurt Sauce, 76
　Creamy Horseradish Sauce, 119
　Grilled Fruit over Yogurt, 26
　Grilled-Fruit Parfait, 187
　Grilled Salmon "Eggs Benedict" over Sweet Potato
　　Latkes, 24–25
　Healthy Caesar Salad with Grilled Romaine, 61
　Mushroom Sauce, 172–173
Green Bean Pesto, 133
Green bell peppers
　Asian-Style Grill-Top Stir-Fry, 148
　Chicken Fajita, 100–101
　Garden Veggie Antipasto, 62–63
　Grilled Sardines over Greek Salad, 59
　Sirloin Carnitas with Chili-Lime Sour Cream, 117
Green Curry, 85
Grilled-and-Stuffed Potato Skins, 51
Grilled Angel Food Cake S'Mores, 185
Grilled Apple Cobbler, 184
Grilled Apple Stuffed with Oatmeal, 22
Grilled Bananas, 178–179
Grilled-Beet Carpaccio, 40
Grilled-Beet Salad with Balsamic Pesto, 57
Grilled Breakfast Pizza, 32–33
Grilled Broccolini, 155
Grilled Chicken Salad, 98
Grilled Clams with Spinach and Celery, 87
Grilled Corn and Tomato Salad, 67
Grilled Crab Cakes, 42
Grilled Edamame with Soy-Miso Glaze, 39
Grilled Figs with Orange Balsamic Glaze, Mascarpone,
　and Slivered Almonds, 182
Grilled Fruit over Yogurt, 26
Grilled-Fruit Parfait, 187
Grilled Mushroom Lettuce Wraps, 45–46
Grilled Oysters with White-Wine-and-Bell-Pepper
　Mignonette Sauce, 75
Grilled-Peach Melba, 183
Grilled Peanut-Butter-and-Banana Sandwiches, 28
Grilled Pineapple, 186
Grilled Salmon "Eggs Benedict" over Sweet Potato

Latkes, 24–25
Grilled Sardines over Greek Salad, 59
Grilled Scallops with Green Curry Lentils, 85
Grilled Seafood Paella, 74
Grilled Steak and Eggs, 27
Grilled Strawberries with Balsamic Port Glaze, Blue
　Cheese, and Walnuts, 181
Grilled Sweet-Potato "Fries," 166
Grilled-Tomato Soup, 159
Grilled Turkey Chorizo Chilaquiles, 20–21
Grilled-Watermelon and Watercress Salad, 64
Grills, 6–7
Grill-Top Baked Eggs with Salsa, 29
Grill-Top Baked Potato, 168
Grill-Top Baked Spinach, 161
Grill-Top Black-eyed Peas, 171
Grill-Top Lentils, 170
Grill-Top Tomato and Parmesan, 150
Grill-Top Vegetable Frittata, 23
Guacamole
　Arctic Char with Pepper Guacamole, 72
　Guacamole-Style Edamame, 41

H
Habanero pepper
　Lettuce Wraps of Grilled Tofu and Moroccan
　　Couscous with Spicy Tomato Chutney, 50
Ham
　Cervena Venison Medallions with Pancetta,
　　Toasted-Fennel-Seed Crust, Grilled Summer
　　Vegetables, and Walnut Pesto, 112–113
Hardy, Maxcell, 165
Healthy Caesar Salad with Grilled Romaine, 61
Hollandaise Sauce, 25
Homocysteine, 19
Honey-Mustard BBQ Turkey, 94
Horseradish, 119
Hummus, 47
　Pepper-and-Garlic Hummus, 47
Hydration, watermelon and, 64

I
Iceberg lettuce
　Philippine-Inspired Pork Lettuce Wraps, 123

J
Jalapeño peppers
　Duck with Plum Sauce, 106
　Lemongrass Shrimp Lollipops, 79
　Philippine-Inspired Pork Lettuce Wraps, 123
　Vegetable-and-Scallop Ceviche, 84
Jelly, Red-Pepper, 125
Jicama, 109
　Ostrich with Jicama Slaw, 109

K
Kale, Braised, 151
Karmel, Elizabeth, 178
Kebabs, Roasted-Garlic-and-Balsamic-Marinated
　Vegetable, 152–153
Kefir
　Tequila-and-Lime Kefir Sauce, 37
Knives, 11
Korean-Style Chicken Lettuce Wraps, 46

L
Lactose-free goat cheese, 48
Lamb
　Mustard-and-Mint Ground Lamb with Feta-
　　Yogurt Sauce, 134
　Rack of Lamb with Sour Red-Pepper Jell, 125
　Wasabi-Spice Rack of Lamb, 126
Latkes, Grilled Salmon "Eggs Benedict" over Sweet
　Potato, 24–25
Leeks
　Brown-Sugar-and-White-Balsamic-Glazed Root
　　Vegetables, 165
Lemongrass
　Grilled Scallops with Green Curry Lentils, 85
　Lemongrass Shrimp "Lollipops," 79
Lentils
　Grilled Scallops with Green Curry Lentils, 85
　Grilled Scrambled Tofu with Potato, Lentil, and
　　Sweet Onion Hash, 30–31
　Grill-Top Lentils, 170
　Vegetarian Lentil Slider, 140
Lettuce. See also Bibb lettuce; Iceberg lettuce;
　Romaine lettuce
　Lettuce Wraps of Grilled Tofu and Moroccan

Couscous with Spicy Tomato Churney, 50
Lobster
Ginger Grilled Lobster, 70–71
Lutein, 24, 144
Lycopene, 143, 159
Lysine, 169

M

Mangoes
Chicken Meatball Kebobs with Mango-Papaya Sauce, 103
Fiery Mango Dipping Sauce, 38
Fruit Salsa, 141
Sea Bass with Tropical Salsa, 78
Maple-Butternut-Squash Sauce, 95
Marinades, 8–9
for Korean-Style Chicken Lettuce Wraps, 46
for Roasted-Garlic-and-Balsamic Marinated Vegetable Kebabs, 153
for Ultimate Portobello Slider, 139
for Warm Flank Steak, Tomato, and Asparagus Salad, 58
Meat, 110–127. See also Beef; Lamb; Pork
See also Cervena venison
Meatballs, Turkey-and-Coconut, with Spicy Peanut Sauce, 93
Mediterranean Whole Fish with Tomato-Artichoke Bruschetta, 80–81
Metabolic syndrome, risk of developing, 19
Mignonette Sauce, 75
Mixed Mushrooms, 158
Mora, Jeff, 20
Moroccan Grilled Fennel Salad, 54–55
Mushrooms, 158. See also Shitake mushrooms
Cervena Venison Medallions with Pancetta, Toasted-Fennel-Seed Crust, Grilled Summer Vegetables, and Walnut Pesto, 112–113
Mixed Mushrooms, 158
Polenta with Creamy Mushroom Sauce, 172–173
Roasted-Garlic-and-Balsamic-Marinated Vegetable Kebabs, 152–153
Mussels
Grilled Seafood Paella, 74
MyPlate.gov, 53

N

Napa cabbage
Asian-Style Grill-Top Stir-Fry, 148
Balsamic-Glazed Cervena Kebabs with Sweet Peppers, Cipollini Onions, and Fennel Slaw, 116
National Weight Control Registry (NWCR), 17
Nectarines
Grilled-Fruit Parfait, 187
Non-alcoholic drinks, 13

O

Oatmeal, Grilled Apple Stuffed with, 22
Obesity, appetizers as cause of, 35
Olive oil, 66
Omega-3 fatty acids, 59, 69, 130
Onions. See also Red onions
Chicken Fajita, 100–101
Grilled Scrambled Tofu with Potato, Lentil, and Sweet Onion Hash, 30–31
Grill-Top Black-eyed Peas, 171
Grill-Top Lentils, 170
Sherry Vinegar Onions, 136
Sirloin Carnitas with Chili-Lime Sour Cream, 117
Wheat-Berry-and-Grilled-Vegetable Tabbouleh, 174
Orange Balsamic Glaze, 182
Orange bell peppers
Roasted-Garlic-and-Balsamic-Marinated Vegetable Kebabs, 152–153
Orange-Glazed Acorn Squash, 167
Oranges
Fiery Mango Dipping Sauce, 38
Moroccan Grilled-Fennel Salad, 55
Oregano, 10, 80
Ostrich, 89
Ostrich Open-Faced Sandwich with Sundried Tomatoes and Chimichurri Sauce, 107–108
Ostrich with Jicama Slaw, 109
Oysters, 75
Grilled Oysters with White-Wine-and-Bell-Pepper Mignonette Sauce, 75

P

Pablano peppers
Grilled-and-Stuffed Potato Skins, 51

Paella, Grilled Seafood, 74
Pahk, Peter, 35
Papaya, 103
Chicken Meatball Kebobs with Mango-Papaya Sauce, 103
Fruit Salsa, 141
Paprika, 10
Peaches, 183
Grilled Fruit over Yogurt, 26
Grilled-Peach Melba, 183
Peanut butter
Grilled Peanut-Butter-and-Banana Sandwiches, 28
Skirt Steak with Pepper Chimichurri Sauce, 120
Turkey-and-Coconut Meatballs with Spicy Peanut Sauce, 93
Pears
Arugula-and-Roquefort-Stuffed Pork Chops, 124
Pepper-and-Garlic Hummus, 47
Pepper Chimichurri Sauce, 120
Pesto, Green Bean, 133
Phytonutrients, 80, 143, 164
Pickled Beets, 136
Pineapple
Grilled Fruit over Yogurt, 26
Grilled Pineapple, 186
Korean-Style Chicken Lettuce Wraps, 46
Sea Bass with Tropical Salsa, 78
Pizza
BBQ Pizza, 146
Garden Pizza, 149
Grilled Breakfast Pizza, 32–33
Portobello Pizza, 154
Plate method of portion control, 15
Plums
Grilled Fruit over Yogurt, 26
Plum tomatoes
Bruschetta with Apples and Goat Cheese, 48
Scrambled Tofu with Potato, Lentil, and Sweet Onion Hash, 30–31
Poblano peppers
Chipotle Turkey Tenderloin with Roasted-Corn-and-Black-Bean Salsa, 91
Polenta with Creamy Mushroom Sauce, 172–173
Pork. See also Ham
Arugula-and-Roquefort-Stuffed Pork Chops, 124
Asian-Style BBQ Pork Tenderloin, 121
Grilled Pork with Avocado Salsa, 122
Lean Ground Pork with Asian Slaw, 135
Philippine-Inspired Pork Lettuce Wraps, 123
Portions, 15–17
Portobello mushrooms, 139
Garden Veggie Antipasto, 62–63
Portobello Pizza, 154
Tossed Mushrooms and Baby Spinach, 65
Ultimate Portobello Slider, 139
Potatoes
Balsamic-Dijon Potato Salad, 175
Grilled-and-Stuffed Potato Skins, 51
Grill-Top Baked Potato, 168
Grill-Top Vegetable Frittata, 23
purple, 51
Scrambled Tofu with Potato, Lentil, and Sweet Onion Hash, 30–31
Poultry, 88–109
Brick Chicken, 97
Chicken Fajita, 100–101
Chicken Meatball Kebobs with Mango-Papaya Sauce, 103
Chicken Satay with Fiery Mango Dipping Sauce, 38
Chicken Souvlaki with Cucumber Sauce on Whole-Wheat Pita, 102
Chipotle Turkey Tenderloin with Roasted-Corn-and-Black-Bean Salsa, 91
Duck with Cherry-Port-Wine Sauce, 105
Duck with Plum Sauce, 106
Grilled Chicken Salad, 98
Honey-Mustard BBQ Turkey, 94
Korean-Style Chicken Lettuce Wraps, 46
Ostrich Open-Faced Sandwich with Sundried Tomatoes and Chimichurri Sauce, 107–108
Ostrich with Jicama Slaw, 109
Shredded Chicken with Grilled Corn Cakes, 99
Tandoori Spice-Rubbed Chicken, 96
Tea-Spice Duck Breast, 104
Turkey-and-Coconut Meatballs with Spicy Peanut Sauce, 93
Turkey Drumstick with Apple-Maple BBQ Sauce, 92
Wild-Rice-Stuffed Chicken Breast with Maple-Butternut-Squash Sauce, 95
Prawns
Santa Barbara Prawns with Organic Tequila and Lime Kefir Sauce, 36–37

Produce for Better Health Foundation, 143
Protein, 14, 35

Q

Quercetin, 54
Quinoa, 169
Quinoa and Grilled Vegetables, 169
Wild-Rice-Stuffed Chicken Breast with Maple-Butternut-Squash Sauce, 95

R

Radicchio
Balsamic-Glazed Cervena Kebabs with Sweet Peppers, Cipollini Onions, and Fennel Slaw, 116
Seared Radicchio Salad with Mustard Vinaigrette, 66
Radishes
Brown-Sugar-and-White-Balsamic-Glazed Root Vegetables, 165
Rainbow trout
Mediterranean Whole Fish with Tomato-Artichoke Bruschetta, 80–81
Raspberries
Grilled-Peach Melba, 183
Red bell peppers, 144
Balsamic-Dijon Potato Salad, 175
Balsamic-Glazed Cervena Kebabs with Sweet Peppers, Cipollini Onions, and Fennel Slaw, 116
Chicken Fajita, 100–101
Chili-Rubbed Tuna with Pepper Yogurt Sauce, 76
Chipotle Turkey Tenderloin with Roasted-Corn-and-Black-Bean Salsa, 91
Grilled-and-Stuffed Potato Skins, 51
Grilled Breakfast Pizza, 32–33
Grilled Crab Cakes, 42
Grilled Sardines over Greek Salad, 59
Grilled Scrambled Tofu with Potato, Lentil, and Sweet Onion Hash, 30–31
Grill-Top Black-eyed Peas, 171
Grill-Top Vegetable Frittata, 23
Pepper-and-Garlic Hummus, 47
Philippine-Inspired Pork Lettuce Wraps, 123
Quinoa and Grilled Vegetables, 169
Red-Pepper Jelly, 125
Sea Bass with Tropical Salsa, 78
Sirloin Carnitas with Chili-Lime Sour Cream, 117
Sweet Corn with Red Pepper, Cilantro, and Lime, 145
Red grapes, 118
Filet Mignon with Red-Grape Sauce, 118
Red onions
Braised Kale, 151
Garden Veggie Antipasto, 62–63
Grilled-and-Stuffed Potato Skins, 51
Grilled-Beet Carpaccio, 40
Grill-Top Vegetable Frittata, 23
Roasted-Garlic-and-Balsamic-Marinated Vegetable Kebabs, 152–153
Tomato, Chickpea, and Onion Salad with Grilled-Lemon Vinaigrette, 56
Tossed Mushrooms and Baby Spinach, 65
Red-Pepper Jelly, 125
Red snapper
Mediterranean Whole Fish with Tomato-Artichoke Bruschetta, 80–81
Ricotta Salata Cheese, Fennel, Clementine, and Grilled, Salad, 60
Romaine lettuce
Grilled Sardines over Greek Salad, 59
Healthy Caesar Salad with Grilled Romaine, 61
Moroccan Grilled-Fennel Salad, 55
Santa Barbara Prawns with Organic Tequila and Lime Kefir Sauce, 36–37
Wheat-Berry-and-Grilled-Vegetable Tabbouleh, 174
Roma tomatoes
Chipotle Turkey Tenderloin with Roasted-Corn-and-Black-Bean Salsa, 91
Mediterranean Whole Fish with Tomato-Artichoke Bruschetta, 80–81
Root vegetables, 164
Brown-Sugar-and-White-Balsamic-Glazed Root Vegetables, 165
Roquefort cheese
Arugula-and-Roquefort-Stuffed Pork Chops, 124
Rosemary, 10
Rubs, 8–9
Rutabagas
Brown-Sugar-and-White-Balsamic-Glazed Root Vegetables, 165

S

Saffron, 10
Salads, 52–67
  Balsamic-Dijon Potato Salad, 175
  Fennel, Clementine, and Grilled Ricotta Salata Salad, 60
  Garden Veggie Antipasto, 62–63
  Grilled-Beet Salad with Balsamic Pesto, 57
  Grilled Chicken Salad, 98
  Grilled Corn and Tomato Salad, 67
  Grilled Sardines over Greek Salad, 59
  Grilled-Watermelon and Watercress Salad, 64
  Healthy Caesar Salad with Grilled Romaine, 61
  healthy versus unhealthy, 53
  Moroccan Grilled Fennel Salad, 54–55
  Seared Radicchio Salad with Mustard Vinaigrette, 66
  Tomato, Chickpea, and Onion Salad with Grilled-Lemon Vinaigrette, 56
  Tossed Mushrooms and Baby Spinach, 65
  Warm Flank Steak, Tomato, and Asparagus Salad, 58
Salmon
  Blackened Salmon with Grilled Maple Butternut Squash, 86
  Cedar-Plank-Grilled Salmon Fillets with Mustard-Dill-and-Cannellini-Bean Sauce, 77
  Chive-Pesto-Marinated Salmon Steaks, 82
  Grilled Salmon "Eggs Benedict" over Sweet Potato Latkes, 24–25
  Salmon Slider, 138
Salsa, 29
  Chipotle Turkey Tenderloin with Roasted-Corn-and-Black-Bean Salsa, 91
  Fruit Salsa, 141
  Grilled Pork with Avocado Salsa, 122
  Grill-Top Baked Eggs with Salsa, 29
  Tropical Salsa, 78
Sandwiches
  See also Burgers and sliders
  Grilled Peanut-Butter-and-Banana Sandwiches, 28
  Ostrich Open-Faced Sandwich with Sundried Tomatoes and Chimichurri Sauce, 107–108
Santa Barbara Prawns with Organic Tequila and Lime Kefir Sauce, 36–37
Sardines
  Grilled Sardines over Greek Salad, 59
  omega-rich, 59
Scallions
  Sweet Corn with Red Pepper, Cilantro, and Lime, 145
Scallops
  Grilled Scallops with Green Curry Lentils, 85
  Vegetable-and-Scallop Ceviche, 84
Sea Bass with Tropical Salsa, 78
Seafood, 68–87
  Arctic Char with Pepper Guacamole, 72
  Artichoke-Miso-Sauce-Marinated Cod, 83
  Blackened Salmon with Grilled Maple Butternut Squash, 86
  Cedar-Plank-Grilled Salmon Fillets with Mustard-Dill-and-Cannellini-Bean Sauce, 77
  Chili-Rubbed Tuna with Pepper Yogurt Sauce, 76
  Chive-Pesto-Marinated Salmon Steaks, 82
  Ginger Grilled Lobster, 70–71
  Grilled Clams wig Spinach and Celery, 87
  Grilled Crab Cakes, 42
  Grilled Oysters with White-Wine-and-Bell-Pepper Mignonette Sauce, 75
  Grilled Scallops with Green Curry Lentils, 85
  Grilled Seafood Paella, 74
  Lemongrass Shrimp "Lollipops," 79
  Mediterranean Whole Fish with Tomato-Artichoke Bruschetta, 80–81
  Santa Barbara Prawns with Organic Tequila and Lime Kefir Sauce, 36–37
  Sea Bass with Tropical Salsa, 78
  Sugar-Cane-Skewered, Tequila-Lime-Marinated Shrimp, 73
  Vegetable-and-Scallop Ceviche, 84
Seared Radicchio Salad with Mustard Vinaigrette, 66
Serving sizes, 14
Seyfarth, Todd, 131
Shellfish. See Lobster; Mussels; Prawns; Shrimp
Sherry Vinegar Onions, 136
Shitake mushrooms, 45
  Grilled Mushroom Lettuce Wraps, 44–45
  Quinoa and Grilled Vegetables, 169
Shredded Chicken with Grilled Corn Cakes, 99
Shrimp. *See also* Prawns
  Grilled Seafood Paella, 74
  Lemongrass Shrimp "Lollipops," 79
  Sugar-Cane-Skewered, Tequila-Lime-Marinated Shrimp, 73
Sirloin Carnitas with Chili-Lime Sour Cream, 117
Skirt Steak with Pepper Chimichurri Sauce, 120
Slaw
  Fennel Slaw, 116
  Lean Ground Pork with Asian Slaw, 135
  Ostrich with Jicama Slaw, 109
Sliders. See Burgers and sliders
Smartsizing, 16
Snow peas
  Asian-Style Grill-Top Stir-Fry, 148
Soups, Grilled Tomato, 159
Sour Cream, Chili-Lime, 117
Spices, health benefits of, 10
Spicy Tomato Chutney, 50
Spinach
  Garden Pizza, 149
  Grilled Clams with Spinach and Celery, 87
  Grill-Top Baked Spinach, 161
  Grill-Top Vegetable Frittata, 23
  Spinach-Stuffed Artichoke Hearts, 49
  Tossed Mushrooms and Baby Spinach, 65
Squash. *See* Acorn squash; Butternut squash; Yellow squash
Squid
  Grilled Seafood Paella, 74
Starches, 162–175
Strawberries
  Grilled Fruit over Yogurt, 26
  Grilled-Fruit Parfait, 187
  Grilled Strawberries with Balsamic Port Glaze, Blue Cheese, and Walnuts, 181
Sugar, 163
  Sugar-Cane-Skewered, Tequila-Lime-Marinated Shrimp, 73
Sundried tomatoes
  Ostrich Open-Faced Sandwich with Sundried Tomatoes and Chimichurri Sauce, 107–108
Sweet and Sour Tomatoes, 136
Sweet Corn with Red Pepper, Cilantro, and Lime, 145
Sweet potatoes
  Brown-Sugar-and-White-Balsamic-Glazed Root Vegetables, 165
  Grilled Salmon "Eggs Benedict" over Sweet Potato Latkes, 24–25
  Grilled Sweet-Potato "Fries," 166
  nutrition in, 51

T

Tandoori Spice-Rubbed Chicken, 96
Tea-Spice Duck Breast, 104
Tequila-and-Lime Kefir Sauce, 37
Teriyaki Chicken Slider, 132
Tofu
  Grilled Scrambled Tofu with Potato, Lentil, and Sweet Onion Hash, 30–31
  Lettuce Wraps of Grilled Tofu and Moroccan Couscous with Spicy Tomato Chutney, 50
Tomatoes, 159. *See also* Cherry tomatoes; Grape tomatoes; Plum tomatoes; Roma tomatoes; Sundried tomatoes
  BBQ Pizza, 146
  Garden Pizza, 149
  Grilled Breakfast Pizza, 32–33
  Grilled Seafood Paella, 74
  Grilled-Tomato Soup, 159
  Grill-Top Lentils, 170
  Grill-Top Tomato and Parmesan, 150
  Sea Bass with Tropical Salsa, 78
  Sweet and Sour Tomatoes, 136
  Tomato, Chickpea, and Onion Salad with Grilled-Lemon Vinaigrette, 56
  Wheat-Berry-and-Grilled-Vegetable Tabbouleh, 174
Tossed Mushrooms and Baby Spinach, 65
Tropical Salsa, 78
Tuna
  Chili-Rubbed Tuna with Pepper Yogurt Sauce, 76
  Tuna Slider with Wasabi Spread, 131
Turkey, 89
  Chipotle Turkey Tenderloin with Roasted-Corn-and-Black-Bean Salsa, 91
  Grilled Turkey Chorizo Chilaquiles, 20–21
  Honey-Mustard BBQ Turkey, 94
  Turkey-and-Coconut Meatballs with Spicy Peanut Sauce, 93
  Turkey-Cranberry Slider with Green Bean Pesto, 133
  Turkey Drumstick with Apple-Maple BBQ Sauce, 92
Turkey bacon
  Grilled Clams with Spinach and Celery, 87
  Grilled Steak and Eggs, 27
Turmeric, 10
Turnips
  Brown-Sugar-and-White-Balsamic-Glazed Root Vegetables, 165

V

Vegetables, 142–161. *See also* Root vegetables; *specific by name*
  adding, to ground meat, 129
  BBQ Pizza, 146
  Cervena Venison Medallions with Pancetta, Toasted-Fennel-Seed Crust, Grilled Summer Vegetables, and Walnut Pesto, 112–113
  cooked or raw, 143
  Garden Pizza, 149
  Garden Veggie Antipasto, 62–63
  Grill-Top Vegetable Frittata, 23
  puréed
    Jerk Bison Slider with Fruit Salsa, 141
    Lean Ground Pork with Asian Slaw, 136
    Mustard-and-Mint Ground Lamb with Feta-Yogurt Sauce, 134
    Teriyaki Chicken Slider, 132
    Turkey-Cranberry Slider with Green Bean Pesto, 133
  Roasted-Garlic-and-Balsamic-Marinated Vegetable Kebabs, 152–153
  Vegetable-and-Scallop Ceviche, 84
Venison. *See* Cervena venison
Vinaigrettes
  Asparagus with Mustard Vinaigrette, 147
  for Seared Radicchio Salad, 66
  for Tomato, Chickpea, and Onion Salad, 56
Vitamin K, 151

W

Walnuts
  Grilled Strawberries with Balsamic Port Glaze, Blue Cheese, and Walnuts, 181
  Walnut Pesto, 112
Warm Flank Steak, Tomato, and Asparagus Salad, 58
Wasabi Spread, 131
Water chestnuts
  Grilled Mushroom Lettuce Wraps, 44–45
Watercress, Grilled-Watermelon and, Salad, 64
Watermelon, 64
  Grilled-Watermelon and Watercress Salad, 64
  Watermelon-and-Feta Skewers, 43
Weight loss, 5, 12–13, 14, 17
Wet rubs, 9
Wheat berry
  Wheat-Berry-and-Grilled-Vegetable Tabbouleh, 174
Wild rice, 95
  Wild-Rice-Stuffed Chicken Breast with Maple-Butternut-Squash Sauce, 95
Wraps. *See also* Sandwiches
  Grilled Mushoom Lettuce Wraps, 44–45
  Korean-Style Chicken Lettuce Wraps, 46
  Philippine-Inspired Pork Lettuce Wraps, 123

Y

Yam bean, 109
Yellow bell peppers
  Roasted-Garlic-and-Balsamic-Marinated Vegetable Kebabs, 152–153
Yellow squash
  Garden Veggie Antipasto, 62–63
  Grilled-and-Stuffed Potato Skins, 51

Z

Zeaxanthin, 24
Zinc, 75
Zucchini
  BBQ Pizza, 146
  Cervena Venison Medallions with Pancetta, Toasted-Fennel-Seed Crust, Grilled Summer Vegetables, and Walnut Pesto, 112–113
  Grilled-and-Stuffed Potato Skins, 51
  Grill-Top Baked Eggs with Salsa, 29
  Quinoa and Grilled Vegetables, 169
  Roasted-Garlic-and-Balsamic-Marinated Vegetable Kebabs, 152–153
  Wheat-Berry-and-Grilled-Vegetable Tabbouleh, 174

Have a home gardening, decorating, or improvement project?
Look for these and other fine Creative Homeowner books wherever books are sold

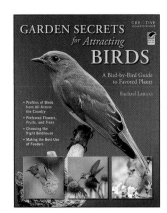

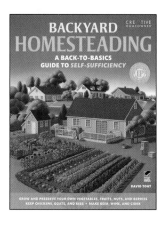